j967.3   Laure, Jason.
LAU
          Angola.

$23.93

DATE			

Reviewed
9KO15

© THE BAKER & TAYLOR CO.

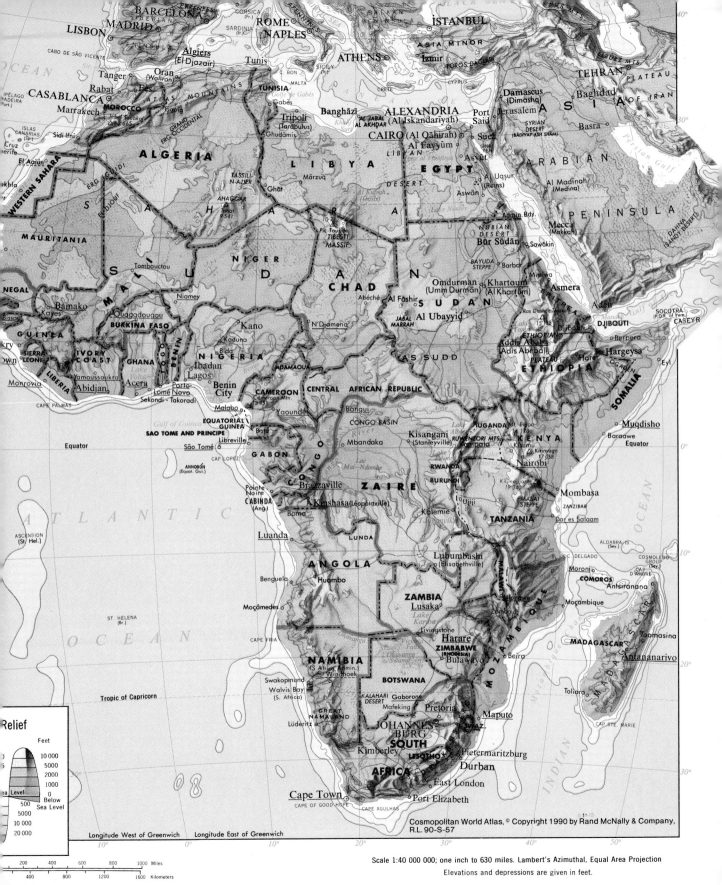

LISBON
MADRID
BARCELONA
PYRENEES
CORSICA (Fr.)
ROME
NAPLES
APENNINES
BALKAN PEN.
ISTANBUL
BLACK SEA
RUS. S.F.S.R.
ELBURZ MTS.
CASPIAN SEA

CABO DE SÃO VICENTE
IBERIAN PEN.
SARDINIA (It.)
TYR. SEA
ATHENS
ASIA MINOR
TOROS DAGLARI
Izmir
TEHRAN
PLATEAU
OF IRAN

Algiers (El Djazair)
Tunis
SICILY (It.)
MALTA
CRETE
CYPRUS
Damascus (Dimashq)
Jerusalem
Baghdad

CASABLANCA
Tanger
Oran (Wahran)
TUNISIA
Golfe de Gabès
C. BON
ALEXANDRIA (Al Iskandariyah)
Port Said
SYRIAN DESERT (BADIYAT ASH SHAM)
Basra
ASIA

Rabat
Fès
Figig
ATLAS MOUNTAINS
Tripoli (Tarabulus)
Gabès
Banghāzī
JABAL AL AKHDAR
CAIRO (Al Qāhirah)
Suez
Al Madīnah (Medina)
PERSIAN GULF

Marrakech
MOROCCO
Jebel Toubkal 13,665
GRAND ERG OCCIDENTAL
Ghudāmis
Al Fayyūm
Asyūt
ARABIAN
Mecca (Makkah)
DAHNA (SANDY DESERT)

ISLAS CANARIAS (Sp.)
Sidi Ifni
El Aaiún
ALGERIA
ERG CHECH
TASSILI-N-AJJER
LIBYA
Mārzuq
EGYPT
LIBYAN DESERT
Al 'Uqsur (Ruins)
Aswān
PENINSULA

WESTERN SAHARA
ERG IGUIDI
AHAGGAR Tahat 9541
Ghāt
Pic Toussidé
TIBESTI MASSIF
S A H A R A
Lake Nasser
NUBIAN DESERT
Admin. Bdy.
Sawakin
SOCOTRA (P.D.R. of Yem.)

MAURITANIA
MALI
NIGER
CHAD
SUDAN
Bûr Sūdān
BAYUDA STEPPE
Barbar
Misiwa
Asmera
Aden
CASEYR

SENEGAL
Tombouctou
Niamey
N'Djamena
Abéché
Al Fāshir
JABAL MARRAH
Omdurman (Umm Durmān)
Khartoum (Al Kharṭūm)
Ras Dashen 15,158
DJIBOUTI
Berbera
Eyl

Bamako
Kayes
Ouagadougou
BURKINA FASO
Kano
Kaduna
Al Ubayyid
AS SUDD
Addis Ababa (Adis Abeba)
ETHIOPIAN PLATEAU
Harer
Hargeysa
OGADEN

BISSAU
GUINEA
SIERRA LEONE
IVORY COAST
GHANA
BENIN
NIGERIA
Bida
Ibadan
Lagos
ADAMAOUA
CENTRAL AFRICAN REPUBLIC
ETHIOPIA
SOMALIA

Monrovia
LIBERIA
Yamoussoukro
Abidjan
Accra
Lomé
Porto Novo
Sekondi-Takoradi
CAPE PALMAS
Benin City
CAMEROON
Cameroon Mtn. 13,451
Bangui
Uele
Mt. Elgon 14,178
UGANDA
Kampala
RUWENZORI MTS.
Kisangani (Stanleyville)
KENYA
Kisumu
Muqdisho
Baraawe
Equator

Equator
SAO TOME AND PRINCIPE
EQUATORIAL GUINEA
Bata
Malabo
Yaoundé
CONGO BASIN
CONGO
Mbandaka
Kirinyaga 17,058
Nairobi
Kilimanjaro 19,340

ANNOBÓN (Equat. Gui.)
São Tomé
Libreville
GABON
CAP LOPEZ
Lac Mai-Ndombe
RWANDA
BURUNDI
MASAI STEPPE
Mombasa
ZANZIBAR

ASCENSION (St. Hel.)
Pointe Noire
CABINDA (Ang.)
Brazzaville
Kinshasa (Léopoldville)
Boma
ZAIRE
Ujiji
TANZANIA
Kalemie
Dar es Salaam

Luanda
LUNDA
Lubumbashi (Elisabethville)
C. DELGADO
ALDABRA IS. (Sey.)
COSMOLEDO GROUP (Sey.)

ST. HELENA (Br.)
ANGOLA
Huambo
Benguela
ZAMBIA
Lusaka
Lake Kariba
Moroni
COMOROS
Antsiranana
CAP D'AMBRE

Moçâmedes
NAMIBIA (S. Africa Admin.)
Windhoek
Swakopmund
Walvis Bay (S. Africa)
KALAHARI DESERT
Gaborone
BOTSWANA
Okavango Swamp
Livingstone
ZIMBABWE (RHODESIA)
Harare
Bulawayo
Beira
MOZAMBIQUE
Moçambique
MADAGASCAR
Toamasina
Antananarivo

Tropic of Capricorn
CAPE FRIA
Lüderitz
GREAT NAMALAND
Mafeking
Pretoria
Maputo
SWAZILAND
LESOTHO
Durban
Pietermaritzburg
Toliara
CAP STE. MARIE

JOHANNESBURG
SOUTH AFRICA
Kimberley
Cape Town
CAPE OF GOOD HOPE
CAPE AGULHAS
Port Elizabeth
East London

Relief

Feet
10 000
5 000
2 000
1 000
Sea Level
0
Below Sea Level
500
10 000
20 000

Longitude West of Greenwich
Longitude East of Greenwich

Cosmopolitan World Atlas, © Copyright 1990 by Rand McNally & Company,
R.L. 90-S-57

Scale 1:40 000 000; one inch to 630 miles. Lambert's Azimuthal, Equal Area Projection
Elevations and depressions are given in feet.

200 400 600 800 1000 Miles
400 800 1200 1600 Kilometers

Enchantment of the World

ANGOLA

By Jason Lauré

Consultant for Angola: Pamela S. Falk, Ph.D., School of International and Public Affairs, Colombia University, New York City

Consultant for Reading: Robert L. Hillerich, Ph.D., Bowling Green State University, Bowling Green, Ohio

CHILDRENS PRESS®
CHICAGO

A family from Luanda, the capital of Angola

Library of Congress Cataloging-in-Publication Data

Lauré, Jason.
  Angola / by Jason Lauré.
    p.   cm. — (Enchantment of the world)
  Includes index.
  Summary: Describes the geography, history, people, and
culture of Angola.
  ISBN 0-516-02721-2
  1. Angola—Juvenile literature. 2. Angola.
I. Title. II. Series.
DT1269.L38   1990   90-2143
967.3—dc20   CIP
                                                  AC

Picture Acknowledgments
AP/Wide World Photos: 37 (2 photos), 44, 51, 55, 83 (left)
104
The Bettmann Archive: 17, 23, 24, 71 (left), 114
Historical Picture Service, Chicago: 31
Lauré Communications: 18, 21, 27, 29, 34; © **Jason Lauré,**
4, 9, 46 (2 photos), 49 (2 photos), 52 (2 photos), 53
(2 photos), 61 (2 photos), 63 (right), 64 (4 photos), 67, 68,
72 (left), 75, 85 (left), 86 (bottom), 105; © **Maryanne De
Leo,** 11, 42 (right), 85 (right); © **Ettagale Blauer,** 13 (left);
© **Marisia Lauré,** 13 (right), 42 (left), 71 (right), 76
(2 photos), 78, 80, 81, 82, 88 (top right), 90 (2 photos), 91
(2 photos), 96 (2 photos), 99, 101 (2 photos), 107
Photri: 14, 88 (top left)
Reuters/Bettmann Newsphotos: 62, 83 (right), 115
SuperStock International, Inc.: Cover, 10 (left), 40, 89
(bottom left & right); © **John H. Ingram,** 5, 10 (right), 86
(top); © **Peter Schmid,** 12, 88 (bottom), 92 (2 photos), 93;
© **Millar Guthrie,** 89 (top)
UPI/Bettmann Newsphotos: 39, 45, 48, 60, 63, (left), 69, 72
(right), 73, 79
Len W. Meents: Maps on 6, 59, 87
**Courtesy Flag Research Center, Winchester,
Massachusetts 01890:** Flag on back cover
Cover: Luanda, Angola—Capital City

An extended family includes cousins, aunts and uncles, and grandparents.

TABLE OF CONTENTS

Cabinda

1	Cabinda
2	Zaire
3	Uíge
4	Bengo
5	Luanda
6	Cuanza Norte
7	Lunda Norte
8	Malanje
9	Cuanza Sul
10	Lunda Sul
11	Huambo
12	Benguela
13	Bié
14	Moxico
15	Huíla
16	Namibe
17	Cunene
18	Cuando Cubango

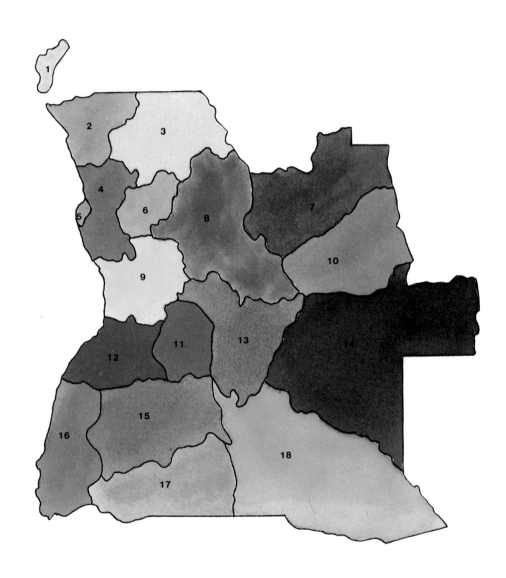

Chapter 1

NATURAL ENVIRONMENT

The sparsely populated country of Angola is situated on Africa's southwest coast. Its huge land area of 481,354 square miles (1,246,700 square kilometers) is nearly twice as large as Texas or a little smaller than the country of Peru in South America. The Atlantic Ocean forms the country's western border, giving it a coastline of 928 miles (1,493 kilometers).

Starting at sea level, the land rises to great heights in the central plateau. In the north, the land slopes gradually upward, but in the south the shift can be very abrupt. About two-thirds of the plateau lies between 3,281 and 5,249 feet (1,000 and 1,600 meters) above sea level, with portions rising as high as 8,202 feet (2,500 meters). The eastern half of the country, not quite as high as the west, is an open, flat plateau that extends into Zambia to the east and Zaire to the north.

Angola is bordered to the north and northeast by Zaire, to the east by Zambia, and to the south by Namibia. Cabinda, a small province of Angola that lies to the north along the Atlantic Ocean, is physically separated from the rest of the country by a portion of the country of Zaire. It is called an *enclave* because it lies totally within the territory of another country. Angola is the only country in Africa that has one province totally separated from the rest of its land.

CLIMATE

The climate does not vary dramatically in temperature throughout the year. It does vary a great deal in rainfall, so the seasons are known as rainy and dry, rather than hot and cold. The dry season, from May to October, is called *cacimbo* and often brings cold, foggy air. The rainy season lasts longest in the north, sometimes for as long as seven months, usually starting in September or October and extending until April or May. In the south, the rainy season begins around November or December and lasts no more than four months. As the elevation increases, so does the rainfall. As much as 60 inches (152 centimeters) falls on the central plateau. The portions along the coast get little rain in any season, no more than 5 inches (12.7 centimeters) a year.

The rain, or lack of it, determines which parts of the country are most suitable for farming and also which areas are the most pleasant for living. During most of Angola's recent history, much of the population was centered in the western plateaus, including the city of Huambo. The major exceptions are the capital city of Luanda and the cities of Lobito, Benguela, and Moçâmedes (present-day Namibe), all located on the coast.

The temperature ranges from pleasant to hot throughout most of the country and for most of the year, although July and August, which are part of the dry season, are the coolest months. Temperatures usually vary no more than 15 degrees Fahrenheit (8 degrees Celsius) within each location. Although Angola's northern border is not too far south of the equator, the Benguela Current brings in cold water from the Antarctic and helps to keep the climate within the temperate to subtropical range.

Angola is extremely well supplied with major river systems,

A young boy poles his boat on the Cuando River in southeastern Angola.

among them the Cuanza, Cunene, Cassai, Cubango, Cuito, Cuando, and Zambezi. Most originate in the central plateau. The Cuanza, which flows from the central plateau to the northwest, empties into the Atlantic Ocean just south of Luanda. It is the only river in Angola that is navigable by large boats. Some rivers are not permanent and flow only during the rainy season. Others are so dependable, they provide the energy for hydroelectric dams that supply much of Angola's electricity.

The country has five natural harbors: Luanda, Lobito, Benguela, and Namibe, as well as the port of Cabinda in the Cabinda

Luanda (left) is situated on a curve of the Atlantic coast. The harbor at Lobito (right)

enclave. These ports were very inviting to early explorers and in large part determined that Angola would be the focus of the slave trade that prevailed during so much of its history.

Temperature and altitude combine in Angola to create a variety of climates and growing conditions. The look of the land and the vegetation change dramatically from coastline to plateau. True desert conditions exist along the entire southern coast, starting from just south of Benguela and continuing to the Namibian border. This is known as the Namib Desert. Here, great sand dunes are seen. The climate is strange here. The hot desert air meets the cold winds coming off the ocean. You can feel hot on one side of your body and cold on the other as you stand right at the shore. A second strip of land, starting almost at the northern

The south has a pleasant climate and enough rainfall to allow vegetation to flourish.

border and extending southward as far as the Namibian border, offers a dry climate but with some rainfall. This dry area, spotted with scrubby bushes, also extends along the lower portion of the country in a zone that runs all the way to the eastern border, but never more than 155 miles (250 kilometers) wide. The rest of the country is divided into two general climatic areas, the north being quite humid, while the south enjoys a pleasant climate, thanks to its higher altitude.

Much of the northeast and northcentral sections are jungles, densely overgrown with vegetation. Few people live here.

Much of the land has sandy soil, making it unsuitable for farming. Only about 6 percent of the land is suitable for farming. The plateaus offer the best climate and soil, both for living and for growing crops. Because the country has such a long dry season, even the areas that have good pastureland in the rainy months offer nothing for animals to eat during the long dry months. Sometimes the rains fail to come at all. A drought in the 1980s led to severe shortages of grain. The whole eastern half of the country is quite flat, with sandy soils.

The magnificent Quedas do Duque de Bragança waterfalls

WATERFALLS AND MOUNTAINS

Several waterfalls are found in Angola including the best
known, Quedas do Duque de Bragança, 344-feet (105-meters)
high, on the Lucala River in Malanje Province, and Quedas do
Ruancaná on the Cunene River, which forms part of the southern
border. The highest mountain peak is Mt. Môco, 8,596 feet (2,620
meters).

Two unusual plants that grow in Angola are the welwitschia mirabilis *(above), a desert plant that lives for about one hundred years, and the porcelain rose (right).*

FLORA

Plants and flowers found in Angola vary widely according to the climate and altitude. Cactus and other succulents grow in the desert regions along the coast near Benguela. In the higher altitudes, various grasses cover much of the land, along with the familiar African tree, the baobab, which looks as if it were growing upside down.

RESOURCES AND PRESERVES

Angola's principal mineral resources are diamonds, found in Lunda Norte Province, and oil, mainly found off the coast of Cabinda and the coastal provinces of the north. Reserves of iron ore are found also in several areas. Small amounts of many other minerals have been found, but little production has taken place. There were once vast forests, but most have been used for timber and cooking fuel. The only substantial forest remaining is in Cabinda and that is being harvested faster than it can grow back.

Mud and thatch-roof houses, called cubatas, *in Luanda Province*

Several areas were set aside as natural preserves and game parks by the Portuguese, among them Kangandala Reserve in the province of Malanje; the Luando Reserve, where by 1961 only an estimated five hundred to seven hundred giant sable were still thought to exist; Quissama Reserve, located on the coastline just south of Luanda; and Kameia National Park on the Cassai River.

Chapter 2

WELL-ORGANIZED KINGDOMS DISRUPTED BY PORTUGAL

ANCIENT ANGOLA

Long ago before the ancestors of today's Angolan population arrived, there were people living in the territory we know as Angola. These earliest people are called San (Bushmen). They speak a language with distinctive clicking sounds in it. They are known for their unique ability to track game and to live in complete harmony with the land. For at least two thousand years these people have lived in Angola, and several thousand still survive there today.

But the San were quickly overwhelmed by the Bantu-speaking people who began to move into Angola from central Africa. No one knows exactly when they arrived. Some believe it was about A.D. 1300, others think it was as early as A.D. 500. The Bantu were

15

Iron Age people who had the ability to smelt iron and make it into tools and implements. This was a major advance in technology and gave these people a great advantage over others. They were able to make weapons that were much more effective than the stones and sticks other groups used to defend themselves.

Their ironworking skills enabled the people to enjoy peaceful and secure lives. Over time, they organized themselves into large, stable, and important kingdoms. The Kongo kingdom was the first to form, starting around the middle of the fourteenth century. The Kongo lived in parts of the lands now called Angola and Zaire. In those days, there was no border to divide people and tribes made use of the land as they needed or until they came upon a different group of people. The Kongo people usually were successful in conquering other groups; they often took in the people they defeated and made them a part of their community. In this way, the original tribe grew and conflicts were quickly ended. About a century later, the Lunda kingdom developed in the eastern part of Angola. Farther to the south, and east of the Kongo kingdom, was a group called the Ndongo.

As the Kongo king expanded his territory by conquering other people, he divided the area into six provinces, each under the care of a subchief. A system of district chiefs and village headman was established, with all of them ultimately responsible to the king. Among the people living in these areas were slaves who had been captured in wars or who had committed criminal acts.

The people of Angola were part of the larger Iron Age community and were developing on their own, without any contact from the world outside Africa. This was their life when the first Portuguese explorer traveled down the coast of West Africa and reached the land of Angola.

Prince Henry the Navigator

PORTUGUESE ARRIVE IN ANGOLA

In the fifteenth century, there was a prince of Portugal known as Henry the Navigator. Henry set up a school at Sagres in the south of Portugal. Under Prince Henry's leadership, the Portuguese roamed the oceans of the world, reaching new continents and claiming distant lands for their king. At Sagres, Henry studied the stars, the only guide to navigation at that time. The Portuguese devised the first tables that showed the sun's position, used to figure latitude, and then invented an instrument, the astrolabe, that enabled sailors to make these observations. The explorations of Prince Henry and the Portuguese sailors gave Portugal the ability to claim distant lands as part of the Portuguese empire. One of these explorations led to Angola.

More than five hundred years ago, Prince Henry's sailors,

An engraving of caravels approaching the coast of Luanda

traveling on sailing ships called caravels, repeatedly sailed as far as the West African coast. These fast, light, round-bottomed ships enabled them to cover great distances with fewer men than other ships of the day. The uncharted seas were treacherous. Men who successfully returned from such trips were like astronauts returning from outer space today. As with Christopher Columbus's trips, the Portuguese were looking for new trade routes leading to the spice-producing countries of the East—and anywhere that promised gold.

Antão Goncalves, the captain of the first trip in 1441, wanted to bring to his king something to prove that he had reached a strange and distant land that no white man had seen before. So he and his crew captured two Africans and brought them back to Portugal.

PORTUGUESE REACH ANGOLA

Goncalves was followed by other ships and other captains, each one venturing a bit farther down the West African coast, and always bringing back more captives. When Prince Henry died in 1460, all he had to show for his efforts were these slaves.

In 1483, Diogo Cão sailed three vessels far down the Atlantic coast and became the first European to see the Congo River (now the Zaire River). After marking his arrival he sailed even farther, leaving a marker 150 miles (241 kilometers) south of the place where Lobito is found today.

The Portuguese had arrived in Angola, the start of a five-hundred-year-long presence there. However, these men were seafarers, not explorers. Their goal was simply to push the limits of their sailing vessels and prepare the way for those who would come later.

SLAVE TRADE BEGINS

The Portuguese quickly moved to establish trade in Angolan slaves. This practice was already an important source of revenue. It has been recorded that one thousand slaves were being shipped from their island possessions off the coast of modern Senegal before Diogo Cão reached Angola. Many of these slaves were transported to Brazil, which the Portuguese claimed in 1500. Prince Henry's idea of exploring Africa in order to bring the Christian religion was not completely lost. Missionaries did travel to Angola and were among the earliest settlers. But whatever good works they performed were far overshadowed by the evils of slavery.

When the Portuguese arrived in Angola, the people were ruled by kings, the most important of whom was the king of the Kongo, known as the *mani-kongo*. The Kongolese saw that the Portuguese, who commanded the ocean, had technical knowledge and skills far beyond their own. The mani-kongo sent young men of his tribe to be educated in Portugal. He associated the mechanical and material advances of the Portuguese with their religion and asked that missionaries be sent to his country to teach his people what the white men knew. He was especially keen to have physicians and medicines from Portugal.

The Portuguese were anxious to obtain ivory from elephant tusks to be used for decorative objects. They also expected to find vast hordes of precious metals. Since they had already established a lively business in trading for slaves, they now had a huge territory that could supply as many slaves as anyone wished to purchase. And they had the beginning of a dream: to establish Portuguese rule right across southern Africa.

But the dreams of both the Portuguese and the Africans were quickly ended. The religion that was tied up with the white man's knowledge carried with it certain requirements that went against the Africans' own way of life. The earliest missionaries were Roman Catholic and they told the Africans that polygamy was against God's law. But polygamy was one of the building blocks of African social structure. However, the greatest harm to the relationship between the Kongo and the Portuguese was the slave trade. Many of the young African men sent to Portugal disappeared, probably taken as slaves.

WORKINGS OF THE SLAVE TRADE

The Portuguese carried out their rule in Angola through a series of governors, each serving three years in office. One of their prime duties was to oversee the shipment of slaves. The Portuguese rarely penetrated the interior of Angola, in part because they met

An eighteenth-century drawing shows the fortress and bay of Luanda as seen from the island of Luanda off the coast.

with fierce opposition. Instead, they established themselves in forts built at natural harbors along the coast, Luanda in 1576 and Benguela in 1617.

The business of the slave trade, finding and buying people from various tribal chiefs, was carried on by *aviados*, agents in the bush (the wilds or the countryside) who had direct contact with the Portuguese, and *pombeiros*, who actually lived in the interior and brought the slaves out with them. The aviados were white and the pombeiros were either blacks or *mestiços*, people of mixed race.

The trade in slaves even included the missionaries who not only bought slaves to use as servants, but actually made most of the money that supported their missions from the slave trade. They collected a fee, called a baptismal tax, on each captive shipped out. Often, the Africans were "converted" in a mass baptism as they were shipped out of the country. For many Africans, this was the extent of their religious education. The Catholic priest could then report back to the church in Portugal that he had saved that many souls.

SLAVES BUILD ECONOMIES

For the Portuguese, the availability of an endless supply of free labor guaranteed the growth of their sugar plantations on São Tomé and Príncipe, their island possessions off the African coast, and in their new and largest possession, Brazil. By the 1700s, it was estimated that a million Africans were in Brazil working on slave plantations. Most of them came from Angola. In just two years, between 1830 and 1832, ninety ships came from Brazil to get slaves. Angola was said to be far more a colony of Brazil than of Portugal. The number of slaves shipped was limited only by the number of ships available.

The cotton plantations of the southern United States made their profits through the use of slaves, some of them from Angola. One of the lasting connections with Africa are the Gullah people who live on islands off the coast of South Carolina. The isolation of these islands allowed them to retain many of the customs and African words from their ancestors in Angola. Their dance and music still reveal their Angolan roots.

Sweet sugar, from sugarcane plantations, was the most bitter of foods for the Africans, for it changed the very way the continent developed. It robbed the villages of their strongest young men and women. While the Mani-Kongo Afonso complained about the effect the slave trade was having on his people, slaves were the only commodity he had to barter for the help he wanted. And so the trade continued.

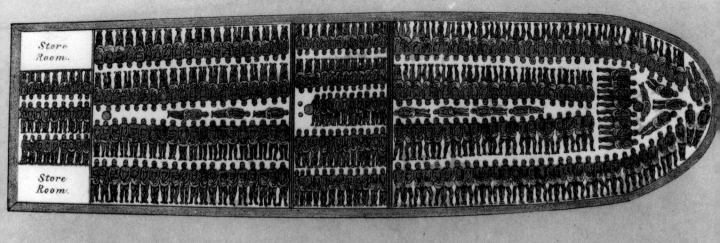

This illustration shows how slaves were packed into the lower deck of a slave ship that traveled between Africa and the Americas before 1850.

For three hundred years, slavery was Portugal's main business in Angola, although the most intensive years of the slave trade were from 1700 to 1850. When slavery finally was outlawed, the Portuguese introduced forced labor or contract labor that was different from slavery only in name.

BRUTALITY OF SLAVERY

A slave *in* Africa was not without hope. Many were domestic slaves from other tribes who had committed thefts and could work off their sentences in African households and eventually become free. They were part of the African social system. The kings who first engaged in the slave trade might have seen it as just an extension of this traditional trade, but a slave taken from Africa and sent away on a ship, in chains, was lost to his homeland forever. The treatment of the slaves sent out of Africa was brutal. They were packed into slave ships lying down, with inches between them, and little space between the decks. The

The upper deck of a slave ship

voyage to Brazil, for instance, took two weeks or more. Many slaves, even the strongest, died of diseases while on board and were thrown into the sea along the way. Young and old, weak and sick were all caught up by the slave traders and had the poorest chance of surviving the trip. Often, the ships were set upon by pirates. In an effort to lessen his load and try to outrun the pirate ship, the slave ship captain often threw live slaves into the sea, even with their chains still on.

The Portuguese were more dependent on the slaves for the growth of their own economy than were other Europeans. While other nations were engaging in trade and slowly freeing themselves from the need to enslave people, the Portuguese remained tied to slavery. This slowed the natural development of both the Portuguese and the Africans. Instead of becoming part of the Industrial Revolution and gradually acquiring advanced technology, the Africans were condemned instead to fill the endless need for laborers on distant plantations.

Portugal saw in Angola a huge land, to exploit any way they chose. One way they saw was to rid Portugal of its criminals. Many of the earliest Portuguese sent to Angola were convicted criminals known as *degredados*. With the exception of the missionaries and the aviados and pombeiros, nearly all the colonizing that took place in the first centuries of Portuguese influence was said to be carried out by these men.

THE KINGDOMS OF ANGOLA

The people whom the Portuguese encountered when they first arrived in Angola belonged to several well-organized and extensive kingdoms. In the northwest were the Kongo, and slightly to the south were the Dembo and Ndongo. The states of the Congo were well integrated into the larger, central African iron-age community. Their unique ability to smelt iron and work it into metal tools and weapons gave these people tremendous power in their community. The Africans, who were constantly engaged in battles with neighboring tribes, greatly valued a fine weapon. When the Portuguese arrived with their guns, the Africans were consumed by the desire to possess these vastly superior weapons.

The Ndongo people called their king the *ngola* and he was a warrior and a blacksmith. The Portuguese applied the name Angola to the whole territory. Throughout the long occupation by the Portuguese the name remained the same, although the European community referred to the territory as Portuguese West Africa.

These different kingdoms began to compete against one another for the benefits brought by the Portuguese. The price they paid for the profits they made was the slave trade.

Not all the Africans were enslaved without a struggle. There were organized slave rebellions as well as individual Africans who managed to escape into the bush where they would find people to hide them. But millions were taken because the guns of the Europeans were by far the greater force.

EARLY RESISTANCE

While the Kongo dealt with the Portuguese, other tribes refused. The Mbundu had lost many people to the Portuguese who needed more slaves for the plantations on São Tomé than the Kongo could provide. The trade between the Kongo and the Portuguese set one tribe against the other, with the Portuguese acting as an ally of the Kongo. The Mbundu leader, the ngola, now found himself fighting against hundreds of Portuguese troops. For a period of a hundred years, from 1575 until the 1680s, the Portuguese fought the Mbundu in their kingdom of Ndongo. They had two goals: to search for silver and to continue the slave trade. The warfare was brutal and bloody and paid off very poorly. The Portuguese never found silver because there is none in Angola and the Mbundu were nearly wiped out.

It took the Portuguese one hundred years to subdue the Africans because the Mbundu refused to give in and because there were so many guns on both sides of the battle. The Africans originally traded their own people for the guns so they could fight other kings, but now they turned them against the Portuguese.

One of the heroines of Angolan history was the Ovimbundu Queen Nzinga, sister to the Ngola Mbundi, king of Ndongo. She represented her people with pride. When she went to the Portuguese governor's palace in Luanda to negotiate, she knew

Because Queen Nzinga knew she would not be offered a chair when she went to the Portuguese governor's palace, she brought a servant who knelt down to form a human stool.

that she, as a black, would not be offered a chair. So she instructed one of her female servants to kneel on all fours, and then she sat down on her servant's back. This dramatic gesture was captured in drawings and revealed how little the Portuguese thought of the Africans. Though Queen Nzinga was successful in her dealings with this governor, eventually the Portuguese conquered the Mbundu people. Following this period of fierce resistance, it would take another three hundred years before the Angolans were completely rid of the Portuguese.

EARLY SETTLERS

Apart from traders and soldiers, few Portuguese settled in Angola until the twentieth century. One source noted that in 1845, more than two centuries after the Portuguese began dealing with Angolans, there were fewer than two thousand Portuguese in the territory, "many of them degredados or others seeking a fortune and hoping to return to Portugal as soon as possible." Angola attracted only the most desperate who were willing to take a chance on Angola. It attracted the kind of people who were unable to make a success in Portugal or anywhere in the Portuguese-speaking world.

Portugal established penal colonies in Angola both to rid itself of these undesirables at home, and also to prevent the British from intruding upon Portuguese territory.

The Portuguese hold on Angola was always fragile. Because Portugal was constantly under attack at home, it left the running of Angola to Portuguese governors brought over from Brazil. They were interested in making money from the slave trade.

The impact of slavery on Angola and its neighboring states can scarcely be measured. Estimates of how many millions of people were taken from Africa vary greatly. Perhaps four million were taken from Angola. Even today, the total population of Angola is no more than nine million. The people who were taken over a period of hundreds of years represented the future of Africa. The strength of Africa became the energy of Brazil, and today at least 40 percent of Brazil's population can trace its roots to Africa.

SLAVERY IS ABOLISHED

The slave trade was always opposed by those who found it morally offensive to use another human being as one would an animal. By the 1800s, the first movements to abolish slavery had begun. In 1806, a major blow was struck when Great Britain outlawed the slave trade.

In 1836 Portugal's prime minister, the Marques de Sá da Bandeira, abolished the slave trade in the Portuguese territories.

Huts such as these were taxed to get money from the Africans.

But it was one thing to *say* that slavery was illegal and quite another to enforce the law. That became possible only when the royal navy of Great Britain sent its ships out to confront the slave ships. Although the trade in slaves was outlawed, those already held as slaves remained captive. But the profit in slavery was gone.

With this revenue denied them, the Portuguese tried to squeeze more money out of the Africans. They had already imposed a hut tax on the Africans, which they had paid in slaves. Now the Portuguese raised the hut tax and insisted on being paid in money or in goods. Many of the Africans who had no way of paying the new tax simply abandoned the areas, most of them in northern Angola. The more the Portuguese expanded into Angola, the more people fled the territory.

By 1845, after more than three hundred years in Angola, the white population there was fewer than two thousand. The real work of building up the colony was performed by Africans who were still treated as slaves. In 1858, slavery was legally abolished in Angola. This meant that no more people could be taken into slavery, but it did not affect the slaves already working for colonists on their plantations. Then, in 1875, the remaining slaves were set free. But after this law was passed, most slave owners found ways to keep them working under the same conditions.

Chapter 3

THE COLONIAL ERA

CLAIMING AFRICAN TERRITORY

The Portuguese had long dreamed about linking their two huge territories—Mozambique on the southeast coast and Angola on the southwest—to create a Portuguese empire across all of southern Africa. They also had a stake in Cabinda, and in 1883 occupied the town of Cabinda, north of the Congo River.

But they were being challenged constantly by other European powers whose own explorers and missionaries were in Africa, creating conflicting and often overlapping claims. These claims had to be sorted out to prevent a European war over the largely unknown riches of their African territories.

THE BERLIN CONFERENCE

In November 1884, the European powers gathered at the Berlin Conference to settle their conflicting claims and to establish borders for their African territories. Treaties to define these borders were signed by Europeans, not the Africans who lived

European powers established borders for African
territories at the Berlin Conference in 1884-85.

there. British claims to southern and central Africa put an end to
Portugal's dream of creating an empire across the south, but
Portugal's claims on Angola, Mozambique, and Cabinda were
honored.

Angola was now recognized by the Europeans as "belonging"
to the Portuguese. It was up to Portugal to show that it had
effective control of the territory. There were fewer than ten
thousand white Portuguese in the territory. The Portuguese had
been trying to exert control over Angola without success for
centuries. The colonization of Angola now began in earnest.

PREPARING FOR COLONIALISM

All it took was a signature on a piece of paper to stake a claim
on Angola. Turning the territory into a real colony was a different
matter. Portuguese whites, especially white women, did not go to

Angola by choice. Portuguese with a taste for adventure and a pioneering spirit to match, preferred to go to Brazil. Angola's entire economy revolved around slaves and plantations. It was plagued by malaria and other devastating tropical diseases that made the new colony little more appealing to potential immigrants than it had ever been. Tsetse flies, whose bite causes sleeping sickness, an often fatal disease, were prevalent in nearly all of the colony except the far south.

Since suitable farmland was in short supply throughout Europe, Angola's huge land mass was most appealing. But plantations with crops that would thrive in Angola required many laborers, and slave holding had been abolished. To overcome this obstacle, the Portuguese devised another way to exploit the Africans. In 1875, they passed a law that defined all Africans who did not work for wages as "vagrants." These so-called vagrants could then be forced to work without pay. Forced labor was just another name for slavery. Since the Africans produced their own food, farming was declared "nonproductive" labor since it did not produce wages.

Contract labor was just too profitable to abandon. For each person brought under contract, the recruiters received a substantial fee. The European recruiters earned $35 for each man. The Africans who actually brought the men to the recruiters received one-tenth of that fee. The trade was so profitable it was called "mining black diamonds." The contract labor system destroyed the normal life of the village, taking away able-bodied young men from sixteen to forty-five years of age. Once again, the Portuguese disrupted the natural development and traditions of the Africans in an effort at propping up their own economy.

THE COLONIAL ERA

For all the years that the Portuguese were in Angola, they had little actual contact with the majority of the people. Traditional leaders continued to rule the lives of their own people but the schools were run by missionaries.

Portugal now was obliged to fulfill the promises made at the Berlin Conference by establishing direct rule over all the people of Angola. Their plan was to totally transform African societies by substituting Portuguese ideas, language, and culture, for the cultures and languages that were the Africans' own heritage. Angola could then be viewed as just another province of Portugal, an overseas province. The Portuguese never asked if the Africans wanted to abandon their cultures and traditional ways of living in order to become Portuguese. The Portuguese, like the other colonizers, assumed the Africans would welcome the chance to "better" themselves—to become civilized.

PORTUGUESE RED TAPE

The Portuguese instituted a complex bureaucracy in place of the African institutions and did away with kingdoms that had survived for hundreds of years. They divided Angola into many little administrative districts, with a white Portuguese in charge of every sector. Then by imposing taxes that had to be paid in currency, they forced the Africans to take jobs working for the Portuguese. Many Africans ran away rather than pay this tax. They left Angola and settled in the Belgian Congo (now Zaire) and Northern Rhodesia (now Zambia).

Portuguese colonial officers in the 1930s

To control people's movements, the Portuguese introduced an identification booklet called a *caderneta*, which all adult males had to carry when they left the village. A pass, called a *quia*, was required in order to travel from one administrative area to another. A birth certificate often was needed, for example, when registering for school. But unlike a birth certificate issued in most countries, which is kept and used throughout a person's life, in Angola a birth certificate was only good for six months. After that, a person had to apply for it again—and pay for it again.

ASSIMILADOS

Because the Portuguese saw their mission in Angola as one of "civilizing" the Africans, there had to be a way to prove they had reached this status. A native, called *indígena*, was assumed to be uncivilized. Such a person could become civilized by accepting the

Portuguese culture, and especially by speaking Portuguese. With his proof in hand, a massive collection of documents, he could apply for status as an *assimilado,* a person who embraced the Portuguese culture. This certified that this African had become a civilized person, *civilizado.* Fewer than 1 percent of Africans ever became assimilado.

There were few white women in Angola. In the 1850s, there was one white woman for every one hundred white men, so Portuguese men often married African women and raised families with them. Many Portuguese men who already had wives and children in Portugal had "second families" with African women.

The mixed-race children resulting from those relationships are known as mestiços. In Angola, mestiços may have very dark skin and Negroid features or have very fair skin and Caucasian features. Many are in between, a mix of their white and black parents. Each mixture was known by a specific name. The child of a white and a black was a *mulato;* the child of a white and a mulato was a *cabrito;* and the child of a black and a mulato was a *cafuso.* There was even a different name for a white who came from Portugal—*caputo.* Those who more closely resembled Caucasians found it easier to get along in the white-ruled society. The mestiços were almost all Portuguese speaking and lived like the Portuguese rather than the Africans. They viewed those who became assimilado as a bit of a joke because mestiços did not have to apply for their status. They were born into the Portuguese culture through their white ancestors. One mestiço woman had an African grandmother, born in the 1880s, who married three times, each time to a white Portuguese man. "She said she would have a better house, a *sobrado* house with two stories, and a better life if she married a white, and she did."

BENGUELA RAILROAD

In Africa, where roads are hard to maintain and there are fewprivate cars, goods are carried by rail. In 1901, the first stretch of
railroad was put into operation. Other sections were built linking
up various Angolan cities, but the Portuguese were always short
of funds to build the important link between the Atlantic Ocean
ports and the copper-mining areas of central Africa. Then Robert
Williams, a Scotsman, provided the financing to bring the line all
the way across Angola and into the Copperbelt of the Belgian
Congo. Still, progress was slow and construction stopped entirely
during World War I. By 1931, the final link to the Copperbelt in
the Belgian Congo was completed. This massive achievement,
called the Benguela Railway, gave the Portuguese true access to
the interior of Angola. It would play a major role in the economy
and politics of Angola's future.

UPHEAVAL IN PORTUGAL

Portugal paid little attention to Angola while it dealt with major
changes at home. In 1910, after seven hundred years, Portugal's
last king was overthrown. For the next sixteen years, the country
was ruled as a republic. In 1916, Germany declared war on
Portugal in Europe and in Africa and Portugal was forced to
defend itself and its African colonies.

A major banking scandal involving counterfeit printing plates
very nearly bankrupted Portugal entirely, making it even more
important to derive some income from the African colonies. Even
with contract labor, which cost the colonial office virtually
nothing, Angola was not proving to be profitable. And then, in

Antonio Salazar was prime minister of Portugal for almost fifty years.
Left: He is shown addressing the Portuguese Parliament in 1942.
Right: He celebrated his twenty-fifth year in office in 1950, and
received congratulations from General Francisco Craveiro Lopes.

1926, the Republic of Portugal was overthrown and a military dictatorship began and lasted fifty years, nearly all of them under Antonio Salazar.

In the 1920s, a major diamond field was discovered and mining in the northeast corner of Angola was begun by a company known as Diamang (Diamond Company of Angola). This mine, which employed eighteen thousand African workers, represented the entire wealth of the country. The population of Angola now stood at about three million Africans, twenty-one thousand whites, and more than ten thousand mestiços.

THE SALAZAR ERA

Much of the thinking that ruled Angola and its people during this era was devised by Antonio Salazar, minister of the colonies in 1930, and then prime minister of Portugal from 1932 to 1968. Salazar remained in office for so long there were entire generations of Portuguese who had never known another leader. He closed the country off from the rest of Europe, eliminating foreign influences and investment as much as possible. Portugal went into a kind of deep freeze, with no new ideas and no exposure to other people. Salazar, himself, never ventured outside Portugal. While keeping Portugal for the Portuguese, however, he also was determined to keep the Portuguese colonies in Africa.

The economy of Portugal was so poor the average Portuguese earned far less than workers in any other country in Europe. Many Portuguese emigrated to other countries and to the colonies. Instead of turning to industrial development, the Portuguese encouraged Angolans, as well as new white settlers from Portugal, to farm the land and develop crops that could be sold. The Angolans became growers of maize, while the settlers planted coffee and cotton. During the 1940s, sisal was introduced on large plantations owned by Europeans.

MINORITY RULE

By 1940 only forty-four thousand whites lived in Angola, yet they ruled the lives of more than three-and-a-half million Africans. There were about twenty-eight thousand mestiços at this time who filled some of the jobs in the government bureaucracy. They were always favored over the Africans. The Africans, on the other hand, were still subject to forced labor, which was not outlawed until 1961.

Even the practice of sending degredados to Angola continued well into the twentieth century. It became a scheme favored by the dictatorship of Salazar, who could easily rid himself of political opponents by declaring them criminals and then banishing them to distant Angola.

Nomadic people who live in the Namib desert

FEW WHITE SETTLERS

The number of white settlers remained very low throughout the first half of the twentieth century, reaching seventy-nine thousand in 1950. These statistics do not count the traders and soldiers who added considerably to the numbers. But the black population was increasing much more dramatically, reaching more than four million by 1950. These population figures, in a country such as Angola, must be considered as educated guesses in the absence of a precise census-taking process. In spite of Portugal's efforts to bring new families to Angola by spending $2 million to develop new agricultural areas, only three hundred families, a total of two thousand people, were actually settled there in the 1950s. Many of those stayed only until they could find work in the towns and cities where they were favored over the Africans for jobs, even when they had just as little education. Skilled workers earned up

39

Workers on a plantation bagging coffee beans

to four times as much as Africans doing the same work. In 1951, Portugal changed the legal status of its African colonies from colonial possession to overseas province. The names of towns were changed from African names to Portuguese.

TRYING TO MAKE THE COLONY PROFITABLE

As the economy in Portugal remained very weak, more and more pressure was put on the Angolans to make the colony profitable. The need for labor was intensive in the areas of diamond mining and coffee production, the colony's money earners. Forcing blacks into working on the plantations was one of the worst abuses of Portuguese colonialism. Plantation owners could order the local chief to supply him with workers. If he refused, he would be beaten. Sometimes the police would come and round up the workers. In 1959, coffee was the chief export crop, earning $48,500,000. Diamonds brought in less than half that amount. Those benefiting from these sums were the authorities, the large plantation owners, and the stockholders of the diamond company. The Africans working at the mines earned $25 a year in wages and goods and were considered well paid.

It was only a matter of time before the blacks would figure out a way to take control of their own lives and their own country. But the process that led to that moment was slow, extremely difficult, and marked with enormous obstacles every step of the way.

BELGIAN CONGO GAINS INDEPENDENCE

One of the drawbacks for Portugal was the lack of a friendly neighboring country to lend support to the earliest attempts at organizing. When militant Congolese attempted to rise up against the Belgian colonizers in the Belgian Congo in the 1940s and were defeated, they slipped across the border into Angola. They were captured by Portuguese authorities who turned them back over to the Belgians. Then a stunning change took place. On July 10, 1960, the Belgian Congo gained its independence. Instead of having this huge ally across the border, the Portuguese colonials now faced an enormous black-ruled country that was sympathetic to the Angolans' drive for independence.

NATIONALIST MOVEMENTS

One consequence of the constant drive for plantation labor was a steady flow of Africans into the cities, where they lived on the

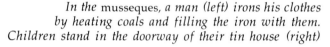

In the musseques, *a man (left) irons his clothes by heating coals and filling the iron with them. Children stand in the doorway of their tin house (right)*

outskirts in slums called *musseques*. They had no leaders to turn to, since the Portuguese had effectively eliminated the traditional tribal chiefs and there was no one to take their place. The blacks knew that in order to have a better life, they had to be free of Portugal and the Portuguese. They were joined in this desire by the mestiços and the assimilados who were among the first to be pushed out of their jobs by the poor whites who were flooding into Angola.

But how could the Angolans begin to talk about independence for Angola when the Portuguese controlled the press, and when it was illegal to form political parties? The answer rested in a few, courageous Angolans who began to organize underground movements both in Angola and in Portugal where some Angolans were attending the university. They had to be very careful in what they wrote, since communication in Angola—press, radio, books, even pamphlets—was censored by the government. Since nothing could be published in an African language, they wrote in

Portuguese. Among them was a medical student named Agostinho Neto, destined to become Angola's first president. The Portuguese insistence on the use of their language proved to be one of the most important tools for the nationalist movements. It gave the various people of Angola a way to talk to each other. Portuguese, the language of colonialism, became the language that helped lead to independence.

In 1956, a group called the *Movimento Popular de Libertação de Angola* was formed out of the despair of the musseques of Luanda. The Portuguese name means "Popular Movement for the Liberation of Angola," called simply the MPLA. This was the first of three important liberation movements in Angola. The leaders and members of this and other liberation movements were quickly arrested by the Portuguese Secret Police, known as PIDE. Many of the key members slipped across the Angolan border into the Belgian Congo, where they were helped by sympathetic Africans trying to achieve their own independence.

AGOSTINHO NETO

The only election Agostinho Neto ever won in Angola was president of MPLA. He was born near Luanda and was a member of the Mbundu people. His father was a Methodist pastor, his mother a teacher and through a series of scholarships, Neto was able to complete his secondary education. After working in Luanda for three years, he traveled to Lisbon on another scholarship and trained to be a doctor. But his efforts to free Angola from the Portuguese were as important to him as his medical studies and this often landed him in jail, the first time in 1951. He was jailed repeatedly after that, but managed to complete

Dr. Agostinho Neto

his studies in 1959. Once back in Luanda, he again was arrested in 1960.

After the independence of the Republic of the Congo, more than 100,000 Angolans fled over the border into that country. Meanwhile, Portuguese immigrants kept pouring into Angola. By 1960, the whites totaled 179,000.

ANGOLANS SEEK SUPPORT

Portugal was voted into the United Nations in 1955, although its colonial policies were a direct violation of the UN charter. United States Secretary of State John Foster Dulles expressed approval of its "overseas" provinces. When Agostinho Neto asked Dulles for help in his fight for Angolan independence, he was turned down since the United States and Portugal were allies. Neto then turned to the Soviet Union for help. This was the beginning of Angola's shift toward a Socialist government.

In 1961 the Portuguese had to form their own militia to protect coffee workers and the coffee crop from Angolan rebels.

THE FIGHTING BEGINS

The violent phase of Angola's struggle for independence began on February 4, 1961 when MPLA members tried to free political prisoners from the central prison in Luanda. They were unsuccessful and the Portuguese responded with heavy force and killed an untold number of Africans. Five weeks later, for the first time, a coffee plantation was attacked in the remote northern area of Angola. Led by Holden Roberto and his nationalist group known as FNLA, Bakongo tribesmen attacked plantation owners and their families. Their weapons were primitive but effective — knives and clubs. These raids were well planned and widespread. In just a few days, several hundred whites were brutally killed. The coffee growers were especially vulnerable since each plantation, called a *fazenda*, occupied a large tract of land in a sparsely populated area. The Portuguese responded with weapons

45

A member of the MPLA youth corps (left), and the MPLA slogan (right). The poster on the wall says, "Victory is certain."

meant for a full-scale war. They bombed villages from aircraft, killing an estimated forty to fifty thousand people, and forcing many more Africans out of their villages and into the Belgian Congo.

The Portuguese army was successful in ending the rebellion and for the next several years the liberation movements staged few other attacks. The three groups were unable to reconcile their differences and unite in their opposition to the colonial government. The MPLA took its strength from the Mbundu people, but was led primarily by assimilados and mestiços, many of whom spoke only Portuguese. The FNLA, who were all Bakongos, were bitterly opposed to the mestiços and assimilados, who they saw as traitors.

PORTUGUESE TRY REFORMS

The attacks seemed to wake up the Portuguese to the real problems they faced in Angola. They hastily began a series of changes in the way they ran the colony. Contract labor was finally declared illegal in 1961, and the government took responsibility for the education of the blacks for the first time. Western nations were invited to invest in the country. At the same time, the government continued to urge whites from Portugal to settle in Angola in order to ease unemployment in Portugal.

Between 1960 and 1974, the number of whites doubled to 335,000. Most of the new arrivals had no more than a fourth-grade education. If Portugal was really interested in improving the lives of the Angolans, adding all of these poor, uneducated whites was not the way to go about it. It was still using Angola as a place to dump problems that could not be solved at home. The few changes made to improve the lives of the blacks were meant to head off the blacks' desire for independence.

AFRICANS WIN ELSEWHERE

But the Portuguese were closing their eyes to reality. Colonies were gaining independence from their European masters throughout the continent. In 1960 the Belgian Congo became independent, one of sixteen African countries to be freed that year. Angola's eastern neighbor, Northern Rhodesia, became the independent country of Zambia in 1964, enabling the MPLA to establish a base of operations there. Portugal was fighting a rising tide.

Meanwhile the independence movements were looking for

A bookstore displays posters of Ché Guevara and Fidel Castro

financial support and backing from countries outside Africa. In
1962, Neto fled to Leopoldville, in Zaire, to avoid the Portuguese
and in 1964 he met with the legendary leader of the Cubans, Ché
Guevara. It was a very fateful meeting. Cuba immediately began
supplying the MPLA with instructors and political support. Their
meeting place was in Brazzaville in the Congo, a nation just to the
north of Angola. By 1966, the MPLA was sending recruits to Cuba
for military training. MPLA received most of its military
hardware from the Soviet Union. Neto had first tried to get aid
from the United States, but the United States was already backing
Holden Roberto's group and refused Neto's pleas.

UNITA IS FORMED

In 1966 the third major movement, *União Nacional para a
Independência Total de Angola* ("National Union for the Total
Independence of Angola"), was formed. It is referred to as UNITA.
Its leader, Jonas Savimbi, was educated in Switzerland and is

Right: Jonas Savimbi
Left: UNITA soldiers demonstrating against the Russian presence in Angola. The sign says "UNITA is a strong party and united it will never be defeated."

fluent in five languages. His people, the Ovimbundu, live in southern Angola, far from the capital.

These men and their movements struggled for independence against the greatest odds. It often has been written that no African nation aspiring for independence was as lacking in training and experience as Angola.

For years the independence movements struggled on, often fighting for control among themselves. They took support from countries both inside Africa and elsewhere — anyone willing to help them. The Portuguese army was committed to fighting the Angolans in a bush war that was difficult to win, yet impossible to end. Each of the movements worked to win support from different areas of Angola, working among the villagers in the rural areas. But there was little genuine progress toward actually gaining independence from Portugal.

PEACEFUL REVOLUTION IN PORTUGAL

As the Angolans struggled to organize and rise up against the Portuguese, a different kind of struggle was going on in Portugal. For fifty years the Portuguese people had been ruled by dictators. Their standard of living was among the lowest in Europe, their economy drained by the effort to subdue the guerrillas fighting against them not only in Angola, but in Mozambique and Guinea Bissau as well. Forty percent of Portugal's budget was consumed in fighting the guerrilla wars.

Unable to persuade the politicians that a military victory was not possible—that the colonies must be let go—a group of young army officers staged a bloodless coup. They forced out the government in Portugal. The new government had no choice but to announce that the African colonies would be given independence. The Angolans did not actually win their war for independence. They never captured a city or held any territory. The Portuguese simply gave up the struggle and Angola was left with the prospect of independence, but without a clear leader.

INDEPENDENCE

The celebrations of the night of November 10, 1975 were glorious as the joyful Angolans awaited midnight and the day of independence, November 11. Among the most jubilant of the people were the Bakongo soldiers who drove their trucks through the streets of Luanda, waving machetes in the air. For this moment, at least, these impressive knives were symbols of peace.

Angolan soldiers wave their machetes as they celebrate independence in November 1975.

A CITY SAILS AWAY

The Portuguese population in Angola had doubled to 350,000 by the time of independence in 1975, half of them coming after 1960. They had come to Angola out of desperation, unable to make a living in Portugal, and they left in desperation, unable to see a future for themselves in an independent black African nation. Along with the poorly educated and unskilled went the skilled and professional worker—nearly every educated person. All but about 6,000 of them simply vanished from Angola by independence.

Crated belongings of the Portuguese were shipped back to Portugal before independence.

The day before independence, on November 10, the last Portuguese high commissioner, Admiral Leonel Cardoso, took down the Portuguese flag and simply left it behind. When the Angolan flag was hoisted for the first time at the stroke of midnight on November 11, there was no Portuguese official on hand to complete the ceremony. The flag had to be mailed back to Lisbon. Unwilling or unable to fulfill the agreement that promised elections, the Portuguese chose not to pass on power, even symbolically, to the MPLA. It was a total abandonment. So ended five hundred years of colonial power in Angola.

The remarkable scene was described by the Polish journalist Ryszard Kapuscinski in his book, *Another Day of Life*. He described the crates that everyone was building to send their possessions back to Portugal. "Mountains of boards and plywood were brought in. Crates were the main topic of conversation. . . . Inside the Luanda of concrete and bricks a new wooden city began to

Left: Portuguese settlers leaving by air
Right: Those who went by ship traveled with their crated goods.

rise. The streets I walked through resembled a great building site. . . . Some crates were as big as vacation cottages. The richer the people, the bigger the crates they erected. The crates of the poor . . . are smaller, often downright diminutive, and unsightly. . . . For materials they use odds and ends from the lumber yard . . . all the leftovers you can pick up thirdhand.''

At independence, there was no elected government in Angola. The MPLA, with its power base in Luanda, assumed control of the government. Agostinho Neto, head of the MPLA party, was installed as president. The government officials who formed the Central Committee, the governmental body that rules the country, were all members of the MPLA. The MPLA *is* the government. No other groups are represented. Neto set the country on a developmental path guided by Marxism, the principles of the Soviet Union.

Chapter 4

INDEPENDENCE AND
CIVIL WAR

AFTER INDEPENDENCE: THE CIVIL WAR

For most countries striving for independence, that exciting day means peace. But in Angola, independence was immediately followed by a civil war. The blame may be placed squarely on Portugal, which played a crucial role during this period.

In January 1975, the three guerrilla movements met in Alvor, Portugal. They agreed to democratic elections in Angola, supervised by Portugal. These would lead to Angola's independence on November 11, 1975. This was the Alvor Agreement. It was meant to assure Angola's future, but in fact it was a fraud. Admiral Rosa Coutinho, who was the Portuguese governor of Angola, presided over the negotiations. But Coutinho always favored the MPLA. The government of Portugal at this time was itself groping its way out of its fifty-year dictatorship. It was not accustomed to freely contested elections and didn't see this as a priority for Angola. Portugal preferred the MPLA, with its leanings toward the Soviet Union. Many MPLA leaders were

Admiral Rosa Coutinho

mestiços and the Portuguese felt more comfortable dealing with them.

Years later Coutinho admitted, "I knew very well that elections could not be held in the territory during the time that elapsed [between January and November 1975] because Angola was still in turmoil. I stated at that time the only solution was to recognize that the MPLA was the only force capable of directing Angola and that Portugal should make a separate agreement with the MPLA and reserve the power for the MPLA on the agreed date of 11 November 1975." And that was how the MPLA took over Angola.

The strategic importance of each faction's base of support was a key factor in determining which group achieved recognition in Angola. FNLA had the support of the Bakongo in the north and UNITA was based in the southeast, home to the Ovimbundu. The capital, Luanda, was the seat of government; all the money and power of the country resided there. MPLA was based in Luanda and supported by the Lunda who lived in the central region. That location put MPLA in the best offensive position. Anyone wishing to rule Angola had to physically take control of the capital from the MPLA. Of the three factions that had fought to gain Angola's freedom from Portugal, only MPLA gained power. No elections have ever been held.

CUBANS ENTER ANGOLA

Before Admiral Coutinho came to Alvor in January, he had already made several trips to Havana, Cuba, arranging for Cuban troops and Soviet-supplied weapons to come to Angola in support of the MPLA. The first of these troops arrived in Angola at independence. Planes that were in position just north of Angola, in Brazzaville, Congo, came into Angola at the moment of independence. The Cubans called this "Operation Carlota." The fighting that followed independence was far more destructive of the people, the land, and the economy of the country than the fight to gain independence from Portugal had ever been.

The Cubans were eager to send soldiers to Angola to help the MPLA because they were committed to the same type of government. With their help, the MPLA was able to score a quick victory and establish a government. But they only controlled the people who were in their own territory. About 30 percent of the land, where the Ovimbundu dominated, was not under their control. Jonas Savimbi, head of UNITA and himself an Ovimbundu, says, "The Cubans have stolen our independence. We should have elections, we should have a democratic society. But the MPLA felt they had no backing of the people at all. They brought in 12,000 Cubans to put them in power."

UNITED STATES IGNORES NETO GOVERNMENT

The United States government was divided about which side to support in Angola. They openly gave assistance to the FNLA, hoping they would defeat the Soviet and Cuban-backed MPLA, but the Central Intelligence Agency (CIA) secretly wanted to help UNITA. The United States Congress was afraid to get involved in Angola because forces backed by the United States had just been defeated in Vietnam a few months earlier in 1975. There was a great fear of getting caught up in another unwinnable guerrilla war. To express its disapproval of the MPLA government, the United States refused to recognize Angola. The Organization of African Unity (OAU) accepted the new government with Agostinho Neto as president.

At the same time that the Cubans were arriving in Angola, the CIA was secretly aiding UNITA. In December 1975, the CIA's role in Angola became publicly known and the United States Senate voted to pass the Clark Amendment, which prohibited any further American assistance. This act, named for its chief sponsor, former Senator Dick Clark, left UNITA without financial aid. The MPLA-backed government had the money from the country's oil production to spend to fight UNITA.

Because Savimbi needed more aid than he was getting from the United States, he accepted help from the Republic of South Africa, a white minority-ruled African nation. To the South Africans, the kind of government Neto was establishing in Angola was the real enemy. The South Africans got involved in the civil war in Angola in order to protect their own interests. The only piece of land separating South Africa from Angola was Namibia, which South Africa ruled illegally. So they secretly assisted Savimbi by providing access through Namibia for the weapons and material being supplied to UNITA by various sympathetic nations.

SOUTH AFRICA INVADES ANGOLA

South Africa also did a great deal more than that. Their South African defense forces actually invaded Angola and, in a *blitzkrieg* through the country, positioned themselves just a few miles outside Luanda, expecting to defeat MPLA. The idea of the governments of the United States and South Africa helping the same cause put the CIA in a political hot spot.

During a fierce three-month-long battle, a small contingent of South African soldiers was defeated and pushed back into Namibia by overwhelming numbers of MPLA and Cuban troops, using four times as much heavy artillery. Then the MPLA troops, backed by the Cubans, defeated Holden Roberto's FNLA soldiers. The combined force of the MPLA, Cubans, and Soviet weapons, forced UNITA out of its stronghold in central Angola. Over months of fighting, Savimbi's forces were reduced until he and a small group of followers retreated into the unpopulated bushland of Angola. By the end of 1976, ten years after UNITA was born, Savimbi was left with sixty-four supporters, most of them women. He began to rebuild his forces, seeking support from his people, the Ovimbundu.

FIGHTING A CIVIL WAR

The war that has been fought in Angola from the time of independence did not occupy very much of the actual land, but it

UNITA forces control an area in the southeastern part of Angola. Their military headquarters are at Jamba.

divided Angola into two different camps. One area was controlled by the government, the other by UNITA. Though morale was high and his people were ingenious at making the best of their circumstances, Savimbi knew that he could not actually win the war. A guerrilla army is not equipped to take over major cities. Other than keeping the Benguela Railroad from running, the guerrillas focused their attacks on MPLA and Cuban soldiers. This, Savimbi believed, would make it impossible for the government to get on with a normal life without including him and his people.

The fighting took place on the battlefront, but there was also a battle for the support of the governments of the United States and countries in Europe, so Savimbi brought people to Angola to see what UNITA was doing and how they lived. Both MPLA and

Both sides have helped destroy the Benguela Railroad. UNITA soldiers examine the Benguela Railroad bridge over the Lumege River after the MPLA had damaged it.

UNITA hired public relations firms in Washington, D.C., to help promote their causes and to establish relations with government officials and members of the press. Savimbi was encouraged by America's refusal to recognize the government of Angola.

Savimbi's followers live in the isolated southeastern province called Cuando Cubango, named for the rivers that form two long borders of the province. This large area, with few people and no industrial development, borders on Namibia. Vast areas of the province are inhabited only by animals that roam freely. In the past, hunters often would come here to hunt for game.

To prove that the government troops were not in control, UNITA forces attacked the Benguela Railroad that runs across the midsection of the country. The line is still largely unusable, denying Zaire and Zambia the most efficient way of shipping their copper out of Africa.

Left: UNITA soldiers gain control of the city of Cuangar on the Angola-Namibia border.
Right: Pro-MPLA graffiti in Luanda reads, "MPLA is the people's party; General resistance."

GUERRILLA WAR

The rainy season is the friend of guerrilla armies. Conventional armies use tanks that cannot advance when the rains turn the land to mud. During this time UNITA would rebuild its strength and recapture territory lost during the dry season. The war shifted back and forth. Sometimes the same town, now empty of people, was captured and lost, and captured and lost again. The slogans of each faction were painted on the buildings as they came through and then painted over by the other side.

But whatever the slogans, people no longer can live in the houses and the people become part of Angola's enormous displaced population. These towns are deserted, the buildings gutted. Grasses and bushes grow up everywhere, as nature begins to reclaim the land.

UNITA depends on sympathetic neighboring countries for logistical support. Traveling to the area of Angola controlled by

Jonas Savimbi with his troops

UNITA meant breaking a few rules, such as not having permission from the Angolan government to enter the country. Flights into UNITA territory were timed to arrive exactly at dusk when just enough light remained to make a safe descent on a secret airstrip in Cuando Cubango. The Portuguese called this area *terras do fim do mundo* ("the ends of the earth"). But it was the whole world to UNITA, the means of its survival.

LIFE IN THE BUSH

UNITA's weapons include some captured from the enemy and some supplied by China. UNITA soldiers are not isolated from their families. They are part of the overall community. Those who are not directly involved with the fighting grow food for themselves and the troops and perform backup tasks. Savimbi encourages the tribal traditions of the Ovimbundu and honors the tribal chiefs. Even after years of living under wartime conditions, the people have not forgotten their real roots.

There is really nothing there to be destroyed through

The civil war makes no distinctions, both blacks (left) and whites (right) have become refugees.

conventional fighting. When a plane is heard overhead, the people run out and hide in the bush. The bombs, when they hit, destroy a hut that takes a day to rebuild. The base camps are moved frequently anyway. This kind of war can be waged almost indefinitely.

DISPLACED PERSONS

This constant skirmishing for territory brought either actual war or the fear of war to much of the country. In many cases, people were forced to abandon their homes and their fields. Many became refugees, fleeing over the borders to neighboring countries where they settled in among people of similar background. More than 300,000 are in Zaire. Another 90,000 are in Zambia and about 40,000 have gone south to Namibia.

It is very difficult to determine just how many people have left their homes and farms. How can one count people who are not there anymore? It is believed that one-and-a-half-million people fled their farms in the rural areas seeking the safety of the cities.

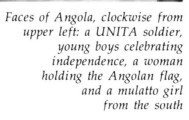

Faces of Angola, clockwise from upper left: a UNITA soldier, young boys celebrating independence, a woman holding the Angolan flag, and a mulatto girl from the south

Chapter 5

PEOPLE AND CULTURE

Angola's people are divided into many ethnic groups, but the majority fit into four major groups: the Bakongo, the Mbundu, the Ovimbundu, and the Lunda-Chokwe. Although there is some overlapping, especially with the dislocations caused by the war, each lives in a fairly well-defined part of Angola's large land area.

OVIMBUNDU

The largest group, the Ovimbundu, makes up about 38 percent of the population. They live in the west central part of the country, centering around the Benguela Highlands, but occupying all or most of six provinces. Historically, the Ovimbundu were active in trade, acting as middlemen during the slave trade. For this reason, they were despised by the other Africans. In this century, many were displaced in business and later in agriculture by the Portuguese who arrived in large numbers in the 1950s. It is estimated that as many as one-fourth of the Ovimbundu men went to work on Portuguese coffee plantations in the 1960s. This came to an end at independence. Jonas Savimbi, leader of UNITA, is an Ovimbundu, as are most of his followers.

MBUNDU

The Mbundu people live between the Bakongo and the Ovimbundu and are the second-largest group, numbering about a quarter of the population. They have a long history of resisting the earliest attempts by the Portuguese to take control of their land and people. Because many of them live in the area around Luanda, the Mbundu have had the most contact with the Portuguese and were most exposed to Western culture. They have lost many of the traditional aspects of their culture, in comparison with the Mbundu people who remained in the rural areas.

BAKONGO

The Bakongo, the people of the Kongo, live in the north of Angola and in Cabinda Province and were the people first encountered by the Portuguese in the fifteenth century. They had a strong system of kingdoms that governed them successfully, holding power over a vast territory that included parts of what are today the countries of Zaire and the Congo. Today, they make up about 15 percent of the population and are the third-largest group in Angola. They played an important role in the first uprising against the Portuguese in 1961, but quickly faded in importance in the war leading to independence and afterward.

LUNDA AND CHOKWE

The Lunda and the Chokwe and other related groups live in the northeastern quarter of Angola. They make up less than 10 percent of the population. Most of the African labor force in the

The Muhuila have hairdos with elaborate decorations.

diamond mines today are Lunda. The social welfare needs, including education and health care, of these people have traditionally been provided directly by the mining companies. The Chokwe were renowned hunters and have long been known for their sculpture.

OTHER GROUPS

Smaller numbers of people make up a number of other groups living along Angola's southern border, often spilling over into Namibia. Nearly all of these are cattle raising people whose lives have been much affected by the arrival of the Portuguese and, later, by the war. Among the most traditional of these are the Muhuila, a group that still manages to maintain much of its culture. The Muhuila wear elaborate beaded decorations and hairdos and live a seminomadic life.

The white population today numbers a few thousand. Some whites stayed throughout the years of the civil war. A few

Mestiços, people of mixed white and black ancestry

hundred came during the 1980s to lend their skills to the developing nation. They come now as partners rather than colonial masters.

The mestiços likewise have been reduced to a small percentage of their numbers. Most, about 100,000, left at independence along with the whites. Although whites and mestiços did mix easily in Angola, there was always an awareness of the differences between them.

The smallest group of all are the San. Though fewest in number, the San are important to the story of Angola. They were living in the territory long before the blacks arrived and have survived all natural disasters, only to be nearly wiped out by the advance of technology, the encroachment of other people on their land, and the civil war. They have always survived in the least hospitable parts of southwestern Africa, finding food and water in lands that appear dry and lifeless to others.

A Methodist Sunday school in 1925

THE FUTURE OF ANGOLA'S PEOPLE

With the huge shift of populations away from the fighting during the civil war, the location of Angola's people today is less clear-cut than at any time in the past. Many have established homes in neighboring countries where there are people of similar ethnic background; some of these people will probably never return to Angola. It will take years before the real ethnic makeup of Angola is known or even how many people make up the population. The current estimate is nine million.

RELIGION

Both Protestant and Catholic missionaries were active in Angola from the moment the Portuguese arrived. Most of the people are associated with a church, usually Roman Catholic. Until 1961, the mission schools were the only source of education for the Africans and the Catholic missions were specifically assigned the task of education. They were allowed to teach only through the use of Portuguese. The Protestant missions, often run by other Westerners, were more respectful of African traditions and languages and, while only about 20 percent of Angolans now consider themselves Protestants, this religion played a large role in educating Angola's present leaders. The United Church of Christ, an American church, has been in Angola for one hundred years.

About 10 percent of the population follow a traditional religion. However, as in many African countries, Christianity is often combined with traditional beliefs. Traditional religion sees the whole universe as a single unit, with the lives of the people living today very closely connected to their ancestors. Religion was a power that resided in the king. He ruled his people's religious life in addition to running the society and having the ultimate say in matters of justice. In the twentieth century, with the power of the kings reduced to a memory, the people turned to the church as the only legitimate place in which to express their desires and their hopes.

TRADITIONAL MEDICINE

While Western medical care was introduced by the Europeans, traditional healing was practiced also. Often the two were combined, especially when a doctor was not successful. A young woman who grew up in Angola recalls her grandmother, a member of the Muhumbe, treating people with a variety of herbs. Many of these herbal remedies are now recognized as quite effective treatments. But when all else failed, then a witch doctor

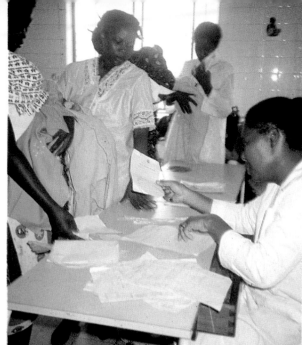

Two aspects of medicine: a witch doctor with a patient (left);
a maternity hospital in Luanda (right)

would be called in to find out what was wrong. Illness, especially
an inborn condition such as epilepsy, was seen as having been
caused by someone for spite. The witch doctor had to discover the
identity of the evil person who caused the illness and then
prescribe the correct remedy. The cure had nothing to do with the
sick person's body. It often involved going into a trance or the
sacrifice of a small animal. Both men and women were witch
doctors.

CHOKWE SCULPTURE

The foremost art form practiced traditionally in Angola is the
sculpture of the Chokwe people. Treasured in museums and
private collections, the exquisitely carved sculpture often takes the
form of ritual masks carved into fierce and compelling faces, or
stools made of human figures. Everyday objects such as hair
ornaments, knives and spears, mixing bowls, and whistles are

Beautiful kambalas *(left), woven of reeds from the river and used as household decorations; young men carving wooden figures (right)*

beautifully carved. A typical Chokwe chair, carved by Ulika Valentin, vividly depicts two typical village scenes. Chokwe sculpture, like almost all African art, is created for use, rather than simply for decoration. All the objects have ritual meaning or practical use.

Many of the finest pieces are now found in a museum established at the diamond mine in Dundo in Lunda Norte Province. It is still possible to purchase an old piece of Chokwe sculpture from an art dealer or at an auction. Some pieces sell for many thousands of dollars, in part because they are so beautiful and in part because little is being made today.

Chokwe basketry and pottery also show the talents of these people. Again, objects are both useful and beautiful, and are made to be handled every day. Beadwork is created by many of the people of Angola, among them the Muhuila.

President Neto speaking at a May Day rally in 1975

LITERATURE

Written languages were not part of the traditional African culture. Storytellers preserved all the knowledge of the culture and passed it along from one generation by telling the history over and over. In modern Angola, the early presence of the missions brought with it a new kind of cultural tradition, built around reading the Bible. While the Catholic missions taught the Bible in Portuguese, by 1893 the Protestants had translated the Bible into the Kongo language. This new literacy led to an outpouring of poetry and storytelling in print, starting in the 1800s. In modern times, the tradition was led by Angola's first president, Agostinho Neto. He was well known for his poetry, some of it written while he was imprisoned for his political activities. He wrote of his hope for Angolan nationalism in 1960:

> Here in prison
> rage contained in my breast
> I patiently wait
> for the clouds to gather —
>
> Here in prison
> rage contained in my breast
> I patiently wait
> for the clouds to gather
> blown by the wind of history
> No one can stop the rain.

His words were so powerful the Portuguese imprisoned him outside the country in a political prison on the island of Cape Verde, a Portuguese colony off the coast of Senegal.

Before independence, Luandino Vieira, Angola's most famous writer, was jailed by the Portuguese secret police for writing about the liberation struggle. Although his book, entitled *Luuanda*, was fiction, he still was considered too dangerous to remain free. Vieira was a white Portuguese who lived in Angola and wrote about the real life of the Angolans living in the musseques. One of his books, *The True Life of Domingos Xavier,* was made into a film. It told of the underground movement in the musseques before independence. The book won a literary prize in Portugal. Mário de Andrade, a mestiço, is know for poetry and works of fiction and for articles written under a pen name, Buanga Fele.

Angola's ambassador to the United Nations, Manuel Pacavira,

Raul Indipwo stands between two of his paintings that have been selected to be reproduced as postage stamps.

has written a novel about the life of Queen Nzinga Mbandi, the amazing woman who inspired her people during Angola's earliest days under the Portuguese.

Each day, a few thousand copies of Angola's newspaper, *Jornal de Angola*, are printed. This lively daily presents both national and international news as well as classified advertisements and full sports coverage. There are games and puzzles as well.

CELEBRATIONS

In September 1989, a major cultural festival was held in Luanda. It brought together artists, musicians, and dancers from all over Angola, as well as Angolans who now live out of the country. Displays of sculpture, baskets, and other works were on view. Musicians and dancers performed traditional works as well as contemporary pieces.

*Victory Day celebrations in
Dondo (above) and Menongue (right)*

On January 8, Angolans celebrate National Culture Day in
honor of the founding of the Union of Angolan Writers. Quite a
different celebration is held each year from March 24 to 27. At this
time, in 1976, the South African army had invaded Angola, and
with the secret support of the United States had moved its troops
very nearly to Luanda. But the United States was forced to
withdraw its support and the South Africans had no other
political choice but to withdraw. The MPLA says it defeated the
South African army and celebrates this defeat. This has become an
important festival, with organized groups of dancers and singers
parading through the streets. May 1 is the occasion to celebrate
May Day, a workers' holiday that has been celebrated by Socialist
countries around the world since 1889. Each November 11, the
Variante festival of popular music celebrates the independence of
Angola.

COMMUNICATION AND ENTERTAINMENT

Western music is heard throughout Angola and was popular even before independence. Teenagers knew the names of groups that were popular in Europe and America. Western films, too, were well known to people who lived in Angola during the colonial period. These were shown with their original English-language sound tracks. Today, Angolan television offers many locally produced news and music programs and broadcasts the very popular soccer games from countries around the world.

Angola has many popular music groups and singers of its own now, among them Bonga, a well-known Angolan who sings ballads; and Duo Ouro Negro, a group of mestiço singers who have created their own special sound by mixing African, Portuguese, and American music together. Their best-known album is called "Black Ground."

Since only about 20 percent of Angola's population is literate, most people get their news and information from television. The television service was started by Luandino Vieira. Many of the programs are imported from Portugal and Brazil, the other major Portuguese speaking countries, but the United States is also well represented. The daily TV guide listing shows Mary Tyler Moore, Tina Turner, and Bob Dylan among the faces seen on Angolan television. Programs from the United States are dubbed into Portuguese.

Movies are popular in Angola as well, and these also are imported from around the world. Since movies are subtitled, only people who are literate can enjoy the foreign films. In addition to action films with Arnold Schwartzenegger, Angolans have seen films starring Jack Nicholson and Woody Allen.

An Angolan runner training for the 1988 Olympic games that were held in Seoul, South Korea

SPORTS

Soccer is the most popular sport in Angola. Boys of all ages play it in the streets, often with a ball they have made themselves out of fabric. People love to watch soccer games shown on television, but very few have had a chance to play on organized teams because of the war. Since few Angolans are able to attend high school, they rarely participate on school teams.

Still many Angolans dream of competing against the best in the world, and a small group was able to realize this dream during the 1988 Olympics in Seoul, Korea. The team competed in the track and field events. Although none of them won any medals, it was a great source of pride for the country and a great honor for the athletes just to be part of the international competition.

Antonio Santos was one of the competitors in track and field. His specialty is the triple jump. Santos had to train entirely by himself, without the advanced training methods or first-rate equipment needed to meet the high standards of world

78

A high school in Luanda

competition. He had no special food or vitamins and lived in one of the musseques of Luanda with his seventeen brothers and sisters.

Angola's basketball team now competes quite successfully in international competition against other African nations. The team travels to neighboring countries to take part in this round-robin competition.

EDUCATION

During the long period when the Portuguese controlled Angola, few students received an education because they could not afford to pay for it. Government schools required students to pay for their books and to buy uniforms. Even some of the whites and mestiços could not afford the school fees or had to sacrifice to be able to send their children to school. All students were taught in Portuguese. This put another burden on the black students, since few of them lived in areas where they heard people speaking

Students in a classroom in Luanda

Portuguese. Not many students were able to stay in school past the age of ten. Graduating from secondary school was very unusual. Anyone who made it through high school and hoped to go to college had to go to Portugal, since there wasn't a college in Angola until 1963. High school teachers were trained in Portugal too, since there were no training facilities in Angola.

The alternative to government schools were those run by the missions. The colonial office made these mission schools legally responsible for educating the blacks. Most of today's leaders in Angola were educated in mission schools, up to the high school level. Those who were able to get scholarships then went abroad to study.

The main subject of instruction in the mission schools was religion. Although the Portuguese government did not contribute money to the mission schools, in 1921 the missions were told they had to teach students in Portuguese, not in a native language.

Primary students using science textbooks written in Portuguese

Education for the Africans was meant to provide Angola with laborers and craftspeople, not doctors, lawyers, or engineers.

It was not until 1933 that the government built its first secondary schools and these only had room for a small number of students. By 1960, the year the war for independence started, only twelve thousand students had reached the high school level and most of them were white or mestiço.

It wasn't until 1961 that Portugal assumed direct responsibility for primary education and that was a year *after* the war for independence started. By 1966 the University of Angola had six hundred students, nearly all of them white.

The children who received an education usually lived within walking distance of a mission school. Schools were more likely to be found in the towns or just outside the city centers. The farther out into the bush one went, the fewer the schools and the less likely that the students, who were black, would be educated. But

A Portuguese reading class in a primary school in Luanda

even those who lived relatively close to town found it difficult to get to school.

Unfortunately, even today, few Angolans attend school for more than four years and the literacy rate is only 20 percent. Since half of Angola is under the age of fifteen, education should be a priority, but that is very difficult in a country that is nearly without teachers. At independence, virtually all of the teachers were Portuguese whites and they fled the country. Only a few Angolans have been trained since to take their place and it will take years before there are enough Angolan teachers.

Many Cuban teachers came to Angola during the years when Cuban soldiers were fighting there. But with the departure of the soldiers, the teachers are leaving too. These teachers added their own language, Spanish, to the confusion. Some Angolans who studied with these teachers were caught up in this language gap, one that separates the generations. One Angolan girl who was taught by Cuban teachers can hardly speak Portuguese and her

The leaders in Angola are well educated. Jonas Savimbi (left) has a doctorate in philosophy and President José Eduardo dos Santos (right) has a petroleum engineering degree.

father has trouble understanding her. A number of Angolans who have spent time with the Cubans have evolved a makeshift language called Portunhol—a mixture of Portuguese and Spanish.

In the areas of Angola controlled by UNITA, schools have been set up also. The government schools and the UNITA schools offer different kinds of education, and very different views of the history of Angola since independence. The problems of education in Angola are well summed up by the different experiences of the president and the rebel leader. President José Eduardo dos Santos earned a degree in petroleum engineering in Moscow, while Jonas Savimbi earned a Doctor of Philosophy from Lausanne University in Switzerland.

This crazy quilt kind of education—first having Angolans learning about Portugal, and then being taught in Spanish, the legacy of the Cubans—has left Angola without an appropriate example on which to pattern its own educational system.

HEALTH

Water, especially clean drinking water, is as much a problem as food for the rural communities—and for the cities too. Many water systems have deteriorated from neglect and the war. When people drink impure water, they are very susceptible to disease. Children are affected most by dysentery, giving Angola the highest infant mortality rate in the world. Of every 1,000 children born, 350 die before the age of five.

Diseases that have been wiped out in many parts of the world are all too familiar in Angola, including cholera, tuberculosis, diphtheria, polio, and yellow fever. In September 1989, an outbreak of cholera in Luanda caused the deaths of 3,138 people. While health officials say it is difficult to vaccinate people in the rural areas against such diseases because of the war, there is no excuse for such inaction in the capital city. Dirty drinking water is the primary cause for the spread of cholera. More than 300,000 children in Benguela have been vaccinated against polio and tetanus by the International Red Cross, but the programs run far behind the actual need.

The most cruel weapon of all are the land mines that have been planted throughout the country. When they explode, they often leave people without arms or legs. No country in the world has as many limbless people as Angola and because there is not enough medical care available, few receive medical attention and even fewer get artificial limbs. It is estimated that twenty-five thousand Angolans have lost arms or legs because of land mines. Doctors from several foreign countries have come to Angola to lend their expertise in this area. Those fortunate enough to be treated at the Huambo Center for the Mutilated are fitted with prostheses, or artificial limbs.

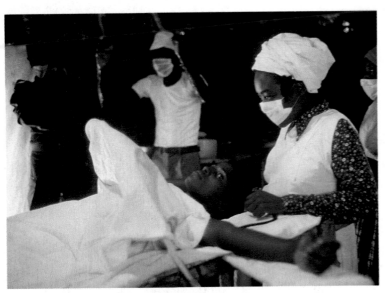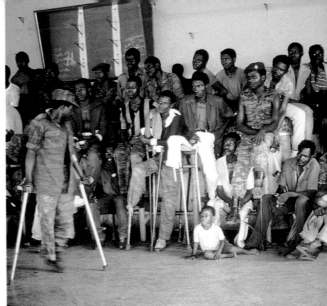

Left: In the bush, doctors perform an appendectomy in a tent. Right: A military rehabilitation center for the many men who have had legs amputated because of damage caused from stepping on hidden land mines.

As a goodwill gesture, in November 1988, five children and one adult were brought to the United States to be treated at United Hospitals Medical Center of Newark, New Jersey. Eleven-year-old Bernarda Ngavulu was paralyzed by a bullet and had come for a series of operations that would make it possible for her to walk again. Twelve-year-old Gabriela Nabomgo had lost a leg while walking to school with two of her friends. The two friends were both killed when a land mine exploded. Gabriela's leg had to be operated on in Newark before she could be fitted with a prosthesis. She and the others were being fitted with prostheses that were more advanced and better fitting than those available in Angola at the time, especially since these devices were able to "grow" with the children. By the time they left the United States a few months later, they were all walking.

Hospitals in Angola are terribly short of supplies and patients are treated under conditions that would not be tolerated in developed countries. Children are doubled up in cribs. Even pain killers are in short supply, adding to the misery.

Above: The tall building in this view of Luanda's downtown and harbor is the Hotel Presidente. Below: Much new construction can be seen in this panorama of Luanda.

Chapter 6

A TOUR OF ANGOLA

LUANDA

The capital city of Angola, Luanda, is a striking example of how independence and the war that followed affect life in Angola. The center of the city features broad streets and buildings in the colonial style of architecture as well as quite modern structures. Gardens line the streets and flowers bloom easily in the mild climate. With few exceptions, however, the buildings have gone to ruin and the elevators no longer work. The paint on the buildings is peeling off. Almost every store is closed because there is no merchandise to buy.

Luanda was established as a port in the fifteenth century and remains the country's largest port today, having a superb natural harbor that can take the largest ships. A long island connected to Luanda offers beautiful beaches for swimming and fishing.

Walls of the fifteenth-century fort of Luanda (above left), the port of
Luanda (above right), and musseques around Luanda's center (below)

Above: A family compound in Luanda with some pigs the family is raising.
Below: A very modern corner of Luanda with a combination gas station, shop,
and apartments (left) and a restaurant with a sidewalk café (right)

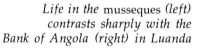

Life in the musseques *(left)*
contrasts sharply with the
Bank of Angola (right) in Luanda

Surrounding the city center are vast slums, the musseques, which existed even before independence. Shacks are built of any materials available and have no sanitary facilities. No accurate number of the people living in the city is available, but it is probably more than one-and-a-half million.

LUBANGO

Located high up on the plateau, nearly 6,560 feet (2,000 meters) above sea level, Lubango is a lovely town filled with the plants and flowers of Madeira, once a Portuguese island off the coast of Morocco. Settlers from Madeira brought the vegetation with them to recreate the feeling of their homeland. Lubango is called "the

Freshly caught fish (left) and locally grown potatoes (right) for sale in the market in Luanda.

living room of Angola," because it is filled with flowers and is so inviting. There is a huge statue of Christ on the top of the mountain. Once a tourist site, today the tourists no longer come and Lubango is known more as the most important southern base of military operations and a military supply town. Because of the military presence, Lubango was spared the effects of the war and remains very much as it was before independence.

BENGUELA

Benguela also is a very old city, founded in 1617. It was an important port during the slave-trade days, since its shallow harbor was deep enough for the boats of that time. In modern

*Left: The buildings in the foreground
house the people who work
in the salt marshes below.
Right: Preparing fish to be dried*

times it has become a fishing center. Large game fish such as marlin, swordfish, and shark may be caught from boats leaving from its harbor.

LOBITO

The naturally deep harbor at Lobito was valued long ago by Robert Williams, who declared that this town should be the terminus for the Benguela Railway. He saw that freight could be loaded easily on ships here, not at Benguela. Fine beaches can be found not far from the town center and fishing here is also a popular sport.

Workmen unloading copper at a rail siding in Lobito when the Benguela Railroad was still operating

GAME PARKS AND RESERVES

A number of game parks and reserves were established by the Portuguese during the colonial era. With the many years of war and the use of land mines, the amount of wildlife remaining and the condition of these is not known. The elephant population is thought to have been greatly reduced by the guerrilla soldiers who sell the ivory to buy equipment. However, they have abandoned this practice, recognizing the need to help conserve the fast disappearing elephant. Some giant sable, an animal unique to Angola, are said to have been taken to South Africa.

TOURISM

Before independence, Angola was a favorite destination for tourists from South Africa and Namibia. The wildlife was plentiful and hunters would come to Angola to shoot animals and bring back their heads as trophies. Angolans would act as guides, taking visitors into the bush and acting as interpreters.

But not all the people went to Angola to shoot the animals. Angola was a place where animals could be caught and shipped to zoos around the world. A famous German animal catcher, Wolfgang Delfs, spent several years living in Angola, gradually acquiring animals that were very difficult to catch. During that time, he made an arrangement with the Portuguese. In exchange for some white rhinos from South Africa, he was allowed to catch roan antelope in Angola.

Soon the war made it too dangerous for catchers or anyone to go out in the bush anymore. Soldiers could hide in the isolated areas where the game was found and the land mines made it impossible to know where one could drive safely. Today, there is no tourism in Angola. Visitors who are there on business must apply for a photography permit if they want to take any pictures at all. Even then, they are stopped regularly as they walk down a street with a camera. The police or soldiers often don't permit a visitor to photograph even after they see the permit. The only kind of visa issued by Angola is for business travelers, but the United States government has issued a strong warning to businesspeople about the dangers of traveling in Angola. When a foreigner arrives at a provincial airport, he must surrender his passport. This enables the government to keep control of the visitor's movements.

Chapter 7

ANGOLANS AT WORK

ECONOMY

When the skilled Portuguese workers and technicians went back to Portugal at independence, with them went the know-how that is the basis for any economy. Angola's economy was totally dependent on foreign skills to organize and run its industries. But the oil industry, which supported most of the economy and was run by Americans, was intact. Of secondary importance was the diamond mining industry run by foreigners from several countries. Although production plummeted after independence, the minerals remained in the ground waiting to be mined. This was not true of Angola's third important money earner—coffee. This profitable crop became a victim of the departure of the Portuguese, who ran most of the plantations. Without them, the crop was essentially abandoned.

An Angolan engineer (left) on an offshore Chevron Gulf oil platform (right)

OIL

Minor amounts of oil were found in Angola as early as 1919, but the first commercial discovery was made in 1955. The most important deposit at that time was located offshore, directly off the coast of Cabinda. In 1957, Gulf Oil Corporation of the United States was given a concession to drill for oil. By the 1960s, this oil field was in full production and Portugal began receiving substantial income from Angola. By independence in 1975, the Cabinda Gulf Oil Company was producing about 150,000 barrels a day from two hundred wells spread out over 200,000 square miles (518,000 square kilometers) of the Atlantic Ocean. For every barrel, the MPLA government received $10.

In 1977, the Angolan government declared that the state, and not individuals or companies, owned all of Angola's mineral resources. The oil industry came under the direction of a government department called Sonangol, but the finances needed for operating the oil fields came from foreign companies, especially Chevron Gulf and Texaco, both American firms. Only a company with extensive resources is able to spend ten years preparing an oil field for exploitation before realizing any earnings from it.

OIL MONEY SUPPORTS ANGOLA

Since that time, oil has provided as much as 90 percent of the government's revenues. Although production was only 130,000 barrels a day in 1982, by 1988 oil production was up to 300,000 barrels a day. New oil strikes off the coast have pushed up production considerably. The price paid for the oil changes according to worldwide marketing forces. Whatever the price per barrel, oil continued to provide Angola with most of its revenues. The prospects for oil production are even brighter, thanks to the development of a second major oil field, just south of the Zaire River. This area is in the hands of a group of European oil companies, including Elf Aquitaine and Agip, and is already producing 150,000 barrels a day. Total production in Angola is more than 500,000 barrels a day. And even more oil has been found offshore both north and south of Luanda, off the provinces of Bengo and Cuanza Sul. More than four thousand Angolans are employed by Sonangol, along with about forty foreign residents. Thanks to the high profits earned from the oil, Sonangol is able to provide its employees with quite a high standard of living compared with most of the rest of Angola.

Sixty percent of the oil pumped in Angola is shipped to the United States, Angola's biggest trading partner. About 30 percent of the oil is bought by European nations and 10 percent by Brazil.

Huge platforms are constructed out in the ocean and the oil is pumped up from wells below the ocean floor. It goes into storage tankers and to the Malongo Terminal, which is located a few miles offshore. Then it is transferred to huge tankers and shipped to refineries. Angola's oil is of a very high quality, with a low sulphur content and is not expensive to refine. A small portion is processed by Angola's own refinery in Luanda for use in Angola. Thanks to the ready availability of oil, Angola is one of the few countries where gasoline for use in automobiles is quite inexpensive.

DIAMONDS

Diamonds were discovered in Lunda Norte Province in 1912. Southern Africa is rich in diamonds, which are found deep underground and also in alluvial deposits along riverbeds. Although diamond mining requires heavy machinery and a big investment to work the underground deposits on a large scale, many diamonds can be found right on the surface of the land by a sharp-eyed person who knows what the stones look like in their natural state.

In 1917, a company called Diamang was formed and given a monopoly to work any diamond fields found in Angola. The funds were provided by firms from Belgium, Britain, and the United States. In exchange for the monopoly, the government of Portugal was given a small percentage of the shares and 40 percent of the earnings, which was later increased to 50 percent.

Diamang quickly became Angola's largest employer of Africans and by 1947 had 17,500 workers. Contract labor, still legal in Angola until 1961, accounted for 5,500 of these workers who

A diamond mine in Lunda Norte Province

earned about $25 a year. Because diamonds are both small and very valuable, security is always a problem at diamond mines. To prevent smuggling, the mining area operated with its own laws and its own security. Access to the mining area was strictly limited. The actual mining was carried on by De Beers, a South African firm known around the world for diamond mining. The company provided all social services, housing, health care, and education for the children.

For the whites in charge of the operation, a comfortable "company town" was built with brick houses and all the services needed. Diamang supplied not only its own power but also generated power for all of northeast Angola through its hydroelectric plant at Luachimo and a thermal plant at Lukapa. The company maintained its own farm, raising pigs and chickens, and also grew rice in the area.

Profits from the mine were enormous, in part because diamonds are so highly valued, in part because the labor costs were so low. By 1936, diamonds equaled one-third of Angola's exports. The value of the diamonds exported increased enormously over the years. New fields were explored and even greater profits followed.

But at independence in 1975, the Portuguese technical personnel departed, as did many of the African work force, and diamond profits dropped sharply. The civil war began in earnest and the diamond mine became the focus of attacks by UNITA, which was able to finance part of its army and buy supplies through the sale of the diamonds. In 1977 the MPLA-controlled government of Angola acted to increase its share of the diamond mines to 60 percent by partially nationalizing the mine.

NEW DIAMOND PROVINCE

In 1978, in an effort to protect the mine and prevent UNITA from continuing to profit from the diamonds, the huge Lunda Province was divided into northern and southern sections. Lunda Norte, the northern province, which included the mining area, became off-limits to everyone but mining personnel. This concept of a "forbidden zone" strengthened the sense of the mine as being separate from the rest of the country.

The attacks continued and production fell sharply into the mid-1980s. The Portuguese technicians were replaced by 240 Filipinos, who now look after repairing the huge earth-moving machines that do much of the heavy mining. Huge scoops of earth are picked up and carried off by the machines, exposing the diamond-bearing ore. Other machines then scoop up this ore, which is carried to a recovery plant where the diamonds are separated from the ore in which they are found. After years of limited

Left: Earth-moving machines are used in mining diamonds. Above: A diamond buyer from Belgium talks with Angolan diamond sorters.

mining and diminished profits, the operation has once again become very, very profitable.

By the end of the 1980s, the mine was producing more than 750,000 carats of diamonds a year worth about $100 million. (The typical diamond engagement ring weighs about one-fourth of one carat.) These diamonds, called rough because they look just as they did when they came out of the ground, are sold to diamond dealers who come to Luanda. They fly in, usually from Belgium, which is still a major diamond center, and make offers for the diamonds that have been mined. Then the rough diamonds are taken out of the country to be cut and polished into gems that can be used in jewelry. Selling the diamonds directly to the buyers, instead of going through a middleman, is much more profitable for the government.

Angola, like other diamond producing countries in southern Africa, is always faced with the problem of how to sell its diamonds. Nearly all the diamonds in the world are marketed by

De Beers, the company based in South Africa. This puts other African-ruled countries in the position of helping to support South Africa's apartheid system. Through the years, Angola has changed this relationship. Now, it looks as if De Beers is moving back in again. It plans to build a diamond sorting building in Luanda to process the diamonds mined in Angola.

Angola has made an agreement with an American firm, Lazare Kaplan International. The firm will purchase about twenty million dollars worth of diamonds a year directly from Endiama, the Angolan company that directs this business.

Even greater profits are possible should exploration ever expand into other areas. Although only preliminary tests have been made, it is known that diamonds also are found in Cuando Cubango Province. However, it would take years of peace and a great deal of money to explore this area to determine if there are enough diamonds to make a mine a commercial possibility. Angola's diamond wealth has just begun to be exploited.

INDUSTRY

Because of the civil war, Angola is faced with rebuilding nearly its entire industrial base. Other than diamonds and oil, very little production of goods takes place. Among the few industries that are presently producing goods is a textile plant in Benguela, which uses cotton grown in Angola. The machinery and technology are French, but the fabric designs are Angolan. Another textile plant is being completed in the city of Huambo. A factory in Lubango makes cinder blocks for building construction.

Several small plants have been established to retread tires. The actual treads must be imported, but the work is done in Angola.

Fixing things rather than buying new ones is a tradition in Africa, where new goods often are too expensive for most of the people or simply not available.

Technocarro, a Portuguese workshop, has been set up with funds from an American bank to repair buses in Luanda. The streets were strewn with the wrecks of buses that were abandoned when spare parts became impossible to get. This company has been picking up these buses and rebuilding them so they can be put back into the public transportation system.

In 1989, Soberi International of Belgium announced it would build a series of processing plants and storage facilities for sixty different types of pharmaceutical products in Luanda, Benguela, and Dondo. Major rehabilitation is starting also on a hydroelectric dam that was put out of operation during the war, repairing the tracks, locomotives, and cars of the Benguela Railroad, and repairing cement factories that were damaged during the war also. But in the south, much of the industry equipment simply lies rusting from disuse.

Portugal is eager to expand its trade with Angola and has plans to aid in several major rehabilitation projects including a cellulose plant in Benguela, as well as vegetable oil and margarine factories. In exchange for this aid, Portugal receives oil from Angola, a guaranteed form of payment.

ENERGY

Many rivers have been harnessed for power, which is created at seventy hydroelectric plants that fulfill the nation's energy needs. Most is used for industry and business; few households have electricity. The chief plants are located at the Cambambe Dam on

Cambambe Dam

the Cuanza River, and the Biopio and Lomaum dams on the Catumbela River. A plant at Luachimo is operated by the diamond mining company for its own use. A major plant at Ruacaná Falls has been out of operation during most of the war. When it operated, it supplied power to Namibia.

The French are funding the rehabilitation of two water-treatment stations that serve Luanda, while Yugoslavia is considering investing in a mineral water plant in Lubango.

AGRICULTURE

Angola, before independence, produced enough food for its own people and a surplus that was sold to other countries. It was also a major producer of cash crops, that is, crops that are produced primarily to sell outside the country, such as cotton and coffee. At independence, the system was changed entirely to one directed by the government rather than individuals. Decisions on what to plant, how much to plant, and who to sell to were all

After maize is harvested it is ground into flour or meal.

taken over by the government. In part, this was done to replace the loss of the Portuguese managers, but also because it fitted in with the centralized planning system that President dos Santos had learned as a university student in the Soviet Union. This system has had no success in Angola for several reasons. Mainly, the people advising the farmers are often wrong in their choice of crops and the methods to be used. The fear of the war and the land mines hidden in the fields made the farmers unwilling to plant more than they needed for their families.

But there were other problems. If a farmer did harvest a crop, the government might not have enough trucks to collect it. Many farmers watched their crops rot away waiting to be taken to market. But even if all goes well and the farmer is paid for his crop, he is faced with a problem that will sound very odd: there is almost nothing to buy with the money received. The shipment of goods into Angola has virtually stopped. The store shelves are empty. So the money does not do the farmer any good. Many farmers have resorted to the oldest kind of economy: they trade what they produce for things that others produce. Cash never changes hands.

During 1984-88, the worst years of the war, the percentage of the population engaged in farming dropped considerably as people left the isolated rural areas for the safety of the cities.

Angola has several different climates that are suitable for growing an unusually wide variety of crops. Some of these are tropical foods, especially maize and cassava, the basic foods of Africa. Maize can be grown over a large part of Angola and is made into flour or meal. Cassava grows easily and the flour that is made from it is very filling. Although it is not very nutritious, it prevents many people from going hungry.

Other tropical crops include sugarcane, bananas, coffee, and citrus fruits.

Crops raised in the temperate areas include wheat, maize, potatoes, beans, and cotton. In the south, which is not threatened by tsetse flies, cattle raising was important but it was greatly affected by the war. The big cash crops, especially coffee, have not recovered from the departure of the Portuguese. The Cubans tried to help out in agriculture, but were unsuccessful. They also followed the Soviet plan, which has not produced results in Cuba either.

In 1989, Angola produced 18,000 tons of coffee, less than one-tenth of the amount grown during its best years. Half the cereal grains needed must be imported. This country, which once produced surplus food for sale, no longer grows enough food for its own people.

The markets, open-air stalls set up in city squares, often have merchandise to sell. These goods and produce usually are bought on the black market, called *candonga*. Angola's currency, the

The black market in Luanda

kwanza, is overvalued by the government, making goods completely unaffordable. But the real value of the money is determined by people who have goods to sell. People in the cities have ration cards allowing them to buy a very small amount of basic goods such as rice, powdered milk, and soap.

FISHING

The area that has been most successful for Angola throughout the years is the fishing industry. Angola's long coastline offers abundant fishing. The big commercial fishing boats were Portuguese owned, although many Africans worked as laborers on their boats. All of the largest boats and many of the small ones sailed away from Angola around the time of independence, carrying their Portuguese owners and their families to Portugal and to South Africa.

African fishermen continue to fish the waters off Angola in small traditional boats, with more than half their catch being sold fresh and used immediately. The rest is processed into fish meal, dried for future use, or frozen. But these processes were interrupted by the war also, and by the loss of the technicians running the canning factories. Two canneries were recently put back into service in Benguela and Namibe, processing tuna and sardines. Much of the commercial fishing is now controlled by ships from Cuba and the Soviet Union.

TRANSPORTATION

At the time of independence, the road network in Angola included 5,280 miles (8,497 kilometers) of paved road and about 16,775 miles (26,996 kilometers) of gravel or dirt roads that were usable through the year. There also were about 22,000 miles (34,405 kilometers) of dirt roads that were really only tracks unusable during the extensive rainy seasons and barely usable even in the dry season. The provincial capitals were not all connected with paved roads.

During the years following independence, an extensive road-building program was undertaken and the road network vastly improved. Unfortunately, many roads have been badly damaged during the many years of war.

Trucks, automobiles, and motorcycles were few in number compared with the years before the war. Many had been taken by the Portuguese when they departed Angola. Many others were not in operation because there were neither spare parts nor mechanics to fix them. Vehicles traveling from one city to another usually go in convoys for greater protection; attacks by rebel soldiers, although less frequent now, still occur. Little travel is undertaken unless it is absolutely necessary.

The Benguela line, the longest railroad in Angola, has been out of operation for most of the time since August 1975, when MPLA and UNITA forces held different sections. Service on the Benguela Railroad has been disrupted almost continuously since then by UNITA forces. Only one small section, traveling eastward from the port of Lobito, is operating.

Until the line is secured and rebuilt, copper mined in Zambia and Zaire must be shipped through Indian Ocean ports, a much longer and more expensive trip.

The line in the south, from the port of Namibe to the city of Lubango and on to the Cassinga mines, has been kept running on a fairly normal schedule, but it too has been hit by rockets and a number of locomotives and other cars have been destroyed. The section that extends farther east is not operative, since it runs very close to territory controlled by UNITA.

Air travel is the safest means of transportation but is quite expensive and severely limited by the number of planes available. The national airline, TAAG, flies internally and also to Portugal. Spare parts and mechanics are a problem for this industry, although help in financing new planes as well as equipment and trained mechanics has come from an American bank. Two new 747s were purchased with foreign financing in 1986. Other airlines including UTA from France; Portugal's own airline, TAP; and Sabena, the Belgian airline also fly into Angola.

A ferry service that was established with the help of Swiss financing runs between Luanda and the smaller cities and points along the northern coast. A new ferry service was opened in 1989 linking Luanda with the southern coastal city of Lobito. Many people take this ferry in order to buy produce that is easier to find there.

Chapter 8

ANGOLA TODAY

THE LONG ROAD BACK

Angola is a nation that reflects its turbulent history. Its kings fought against Europeans. It lived under colonial rule. It fought a war for independence and then it fought a civil war. Few nations have been so stripped of their best people as was Angola, through slavery, colonialization, and war. The strength of Angola was used to build other nations.

In modern times, when Angola might use the money it earns from oil to develop into a vigorous African state, it has instead spent half of that money to pay for a civil war that has devastated both the land and the people. The rest, unfortunately, has largely been squandered on outside consultants and foreigners who have been brought to Angola to provide the most basic services. Instead of training its own people to take over the day-to-day needs of the country, the Angolan government prefers to import Europeans and other Westerners. Today in Luanda, a number of Brazilians hold managerial positions. They, of course, speak Portuguese and so have a natural basis for their relationship.

Under its first president, Agostinho Neto, Angola set off on a developmental path guided by the principles of the Soviet Union. When Neto died in Moscow in 1979, José Eduardo dos Santos became president. Battling both persistent UNITA rebels as well as a devastated economy, dos Santos struggled to find a new way to run the country. There were few people available to help him with that task, thanks to the massive Portuguese pull-out at independence. With few trained Angolans and scarcely any Europeans, dos Santos continued with the Soviet model, applying his own education and the impressions he absorbed while a student in Moscow.

Rather than become a truly independent African nation, Angola turned into a country whose policies, economics, agricultural schemes, medical services, road building—everything in fact—was run or directed by a foreign power. Because the MPLA government was brought to power by Soviet weapons and Cuban soldiers, these two nations continued to play a major role in the development of the country. The very idea of how to run a nation came from the Soviets. State-control of production, central planning, and nationalization of industries were the building blocks of the Soviet system and now they were being applied to Angola. But Soviet-style countries often have trouble meeting the basic needs of their citizens. The central-planning ideas seem to breed inefficiency; products and services become less and less available.

The upheaval in Eastern Europe in November 1989, starting with the opening up of The Wall in East Berlin, and the overthrow of Communist governments, one after another, in Eastern Europe, showed that the philosophy of communism, and especially their economic model does not work. But President dos Santos seems determined to stay with the system. On a trip to Cuba in December 1989, where five Cuban soldiers who had died in Angola were brought home for burial, he met with Cuban President Fidel Castro. Castro proclaimed his intention to follow the Communist line even while the rest of the Communist world was abandoning it.

In Angola, the decision to follow the Communist system was a reaction to the colonial system. Under the Portuguese, the Angolans were not made part of the process of governing. They had no training in running modern cities, in maintaining factories, or in filling office jobs.

The small reforms that have been taken were made so that Angola could apply for aid from the important world financial resources such as the World Bank and the International Monetary Fund (IMF). These funds require a country to show economic reforms. Angola became a member of the IMF in 1989.

ANGOLA AND AFRICA

With its small population of about nine million people and with constant earnings flowing into the treasury from the production of oil and diamonds, Angola has the resources to become a successful country. It is a member of SADCC, an alliance of southern African countries aimed at developing and sharing in each country's resources. Solutions to problems are based on making the best use of traditional methods and resources rather than trying to imitate the industrial countries. The other major members of SADCC are Botswana, Zambia, Zimbabwe, and Mozambique.

This is the way Angola could develop, if it were not for the war.

Instead of rebuilding what has been destroyed, Angola becomes a poorer country with each passing year. The basic services that civilized cultures expect—decent sanitation and health care, reasonable education and transportation—are available only to a few privileged people.

When Angolans go to other African countries, they say they are going to Africa. That's how separated they are from other Africans. Because so much of their country is in the hands of foreigners and foreign policies, they really feel isolated from the rest of Africa.

THE CUBANS

In turning to the Cubans to help with Angola's civil war, and to the Soviets who supplied the weapons, Angola essentially exchanged one kind of colonialism for another. The Cuban presence grew. Over the fifteen years of war, an estimated seven thousand Cuban troops were killed. They were buried in Angola because Cuban leadership was afraid of the reaction if so many bodies were brought back home. But the war continued.

Angola had to house and feed the Cuban soldiers sent to fight and it paid their salaries too. As the number of soldiers increased to more than fifty thousand, the amount paid to maintain them increased too.

Although UNITA at first fought a guerrilla war, quickly attacking the enemy and then retreating to a stronghold, the nature of the war changed dramatically during the dry season, March through June, of 1988. An additional fifteen thousand Cuban soldiers and heavy weapons poured into southern Angola. Their first view of Angola was a surprise. First Lieutenant Vickie

Chester Crocker, former United States assistant secretary of state for Africa

Herrara said, "When we first arrived, we were shocked by the poverty here—the people with nothing to eat, the people in rags." The battle at Cuito-Cuanavale that deafened the countryside with the sounds of rockets called Stalin's organs was described as the biggest in Africa since World War II. The South Africans saw that they were involved in an endless war.

But the war in Angola was complicated by the fight for independence in Namibia, the country to the south. South Africa was using the war in Angola as a way to hide its interest in keeping Namibia from gaining independence.

Chester Crocker, the United States under secretary of state for Africa, had been working toward resolving the Namibian situation for eight years. After preliminary agreement was achieved at meetings held in Brazzaville, capital of the Congo, the final agreement was signed by Angola, Cuba, and South Africa at the United Nations in New York on December 22, 1988. Timetables were drawn up for the departure of the Cuban troops over a period of two-and-a-half years, concluding in July 1991.

Departing Cuban soldiers carry Angolan youngsters in a farewell parade in 1989.

The South African troops already had been pulled out of Angola in 1988. And by January 1990, more than 29,000 of the Cubans had left Angola.

But this agreement did not include UNITA, which sees the situation in Angola as unchanged since 1975 when the Alvor Agreement was signed. And it does not intend to give up. On June 22, 1989 it was reported that a cease-fire had been agreed upon by UNITA and MPLA. The problem is that the terms of the cease-fire were not written down! Everyone who attended the meetings has a different idea about the agreements. The African solution to Angola's civil war was unsuccessful. The cease-fire agreement quickly fell apart and the fighting continued. The United States, which has never diplomatically recognized the MPLA government, continued to send supplies to UNITA, flying them in from Kamina in Zaire. (One of these planes, funded by the United States and belonging to the CIA, crashed near Savimbi's headquarters in Jambe on November 27, 1989, killing four Americans and an unknown number of UNITA members.)

ANGOLA AND NAMIBIA

UNITA's long struggle for recognition and free elections in Angola produced an ironic result: Namibia, which has been ruled illegally by South Africa, achieved its own independence, thanks to the settlement arranged by Chester Crocker. Elections, which had been promised in a United Nations Resolution in 1978, were held, peacefully, in November 1989.

Angola, which has been a member of the United Nations since 1976, has never had elections. UNITA objects to the MPLA government because it was not chosen through elections by the people of Angola and because the government doesn't believe in the Marxist philosophy of the MPLA.

ANGOLA'S FUTURE

The need for national reconciliation in Angola is a view shared by several African countries including Zaire and the Congo, which have been urging President dos Santos to meet with UNITA. The economies of all the countries in the region, as well as the security of the people living there, are affected by the lack of peace within Angola. As long as UNITA is left out of the accords, the whole southern Africa region will remain unstable.

The refusal of the United States to recognize the government discourages American businesses from investing in Angola because there is no American embassy there to help protect American citizens and no commitment to protect American property. It also keeps Angola from receiving direct United States aid. It does not, however, keep American businesses from dealing with Angola.

If peace really does come to Angola, if a way can be found to bring UNITA into the government so that all the people are truly represented, Angola finally can begin to develop its great potential.

With the dramatic changes sweeping Eastern Europe in 1989, the defeat of the Communist parties in country after country, Angola finds itself clinging to an old policy that is not working. Its major backer, the U.S.S.R., has shown itself more and more willing to allow the other countries of Eastern Europe to move away from communism. It seems only a matter of time before Angola must face the fact that the Communist system has not worked and that it must find a better way to run the country and care for its people.

In Angola, an enormous gap exists between the elite who travel around in Mercedes-Benzes and the rest of the population that often cannot find even the basic necessities of life. This is the reason the civil war in Angola still goes on and will continue until the two sides finally meet, face to face.

The situation in southern Africa has changed dramatically. The last of the Cubans will depart in the summer of 1991. The South Africans are kept at a distance by the independence of Namibia. The new leaders of Namibia spent many years in exile in Angola, forming close relationships with the Angola government. The changes in the Communist world, especially in the U.S.S.R., makes them less willing to be involved in supporting a civil war such as this one. All these factors combine to create a positive climate for ending the civil war in Angola since it will now involve only Angolans. What is missing however, is a mediator, a neutral party interested in bringing the two sides together and helping them to agree to end the war.

Map Key

Ambriz	C1	Cuando River	D2, E3	Lungue-Bungo River	D2, D3
Andulo	D2	Cuangar	E2	M'banza Congo	C1
Baía dos Tigres	E1	Cuango River	C2, D2, D3	Macocolo	C2
Bailundo	D2	Cuanza Norte (province)	C1, C2	Malanje	C2
Baixo Longa	E2	Cuanza River	C1, C2, D2	Malanje (province)	C2, D2
Bengo (province)	C1	Cuanza Sul (province)	D2, D3	Maquela do Zombo	C2
Benguela	D1	Cubal	D1	Marimba	C2
Benguela (province)	D1	Cubango River	D2, E2	Mavinga	E3
Bibala	D1	Cuimba	C1	Menongue	D2
Bié (province)	D2	Cuito River	E2, E3	Môco, Serra (mountain)	D2
Buco Zau	B1	Cuito-Cuanavale	E2	Moxico (province)	D2, D3
Caála	D2	Cunene (province)	E1, E2	Muconda	D3
Cabinda	C1	Cunene River	D2, E1, E2	Mucusso	E3
Cabinda (province)	B1, C1	Cuvo River	D1, D2	Mussende	D2
Cacolo	D2	Damba	C2	Mussuma	D3
Caconda	D2	Dande River	C1	Muxima	C1
Caiunda	D3	Dirico	E3	N'dalatando	C1
Calulo	D1	Dombe Grande	D1	N'zeto	C1
Calundo	E2	Dondo	C1	Namibe	E1
Camabatela	C2	Evale	E2	Namibe (province)	D1, E1
Camacupa	D2	Foz do Cunene	E1	Negage	C2
Cambundi Catembo	D2	Gabela	D1	Neriquinha	E3
Camissombo	C3	Ganda	D1	Noqui	C1
Cangamba	D2	Guilherme Capelo	C1	Nova Caipemba	C1
Cangombe	D3	Huambo	D2	Okavango River	E2, E3
Capelongo	E2	Huambo (province)	D2	Ondjiva	E2
Cassai River	D2, D3	Huíla (province)	D1, D2, E1, E2	Otchinjau	E1
Cassinga	E2	Humbe	E1	Palmeirinhas, Ponta das (point)	C1
Catete	C1	Humpata	E1	Porto Amboim	D1
Catumbela River	D1, D2	Kalandula	C2	Quela	C2
Caúngula	C2	Kasai River	C3, D3	Quibala	D1
Caxito	C1	Kuito	D2	Quilengues	D1
Cazombo	D3	Kuvango	D2	Quimbele	C2
Chela, Serra da (mountain)	E1	Lobito	D1	Quipungo	D1
Chibemba	E1	Loge River	C1, C2	Sanza Pombo	C2
Chibia	E1	Longa River	D1, D2	Saurimo	C3
Chicapa River	C3, D3, D2	Luanda	C1	Soyo	C1
Chiluage	C3	Luanda (province)	C1	Sumbe	D1
Chinguar	D2	Luanguinga River	D3	Tomboco	C1
Chitado	E1	Luau	D3	Tombua	E1
Chitato	C3	Lubango	D1	Uíge	C2
Chitembo	D2	Lucira	D1	Uíge (province)	C1, C2
Chiumbe River	C3, D3	Luena	D2, D3	Uku	D1
Chiume	E3	Luiana	E3	Waku Kungo	D2
Cuando Cubango (province)	D2	Lumbala N'guimbo	D3	Xangongo	E2
	E2, E3	Luanda Norte (province)	C2, C3	Zaire (province)	C1
		Lunda Sul (province)	C2, D1, D2, D3	Zambezi River	D3

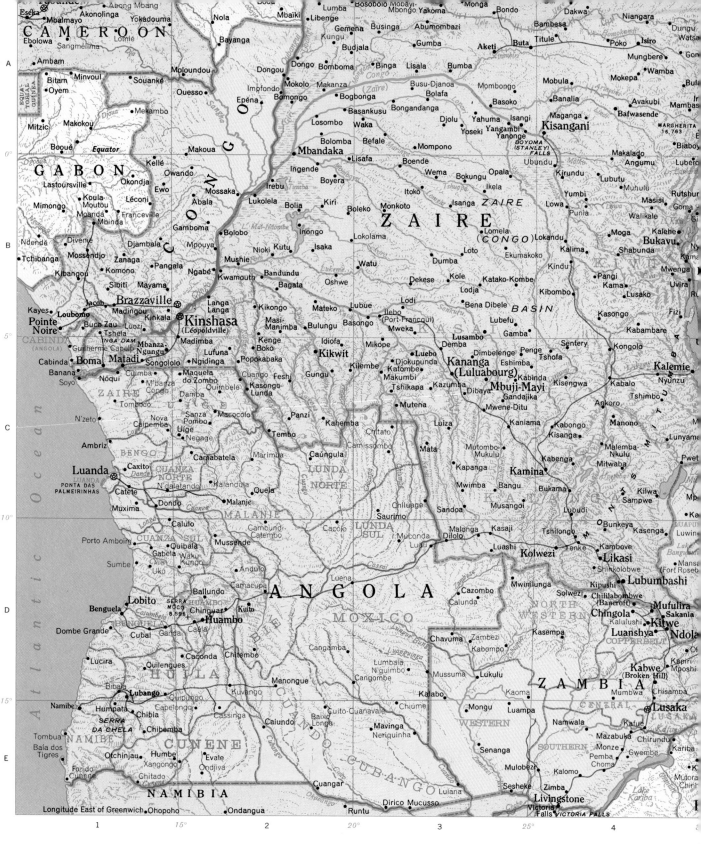

Cosmopolitan World Atlas, © Copyright 1990 by Rand McNally & Company,
R.L. 90-S-57

MINI-FACTS AT A GLANCE

GENERAL INFORMATION

Official Name: Republica Popular de Angola (People's Republic of Angola)

Capital: Luanda

Official Language: Portuguese remains the official language of Angola, although African languages (and their dialects) are used at the local level.

Government: Angola is a Marxist-oriented state administered by the Popular Liberation Movement of Angola (MPLA). There are 18 provinces. The president is elected by the party's Central Committee. The constitution, which was adopted upon independence on November 11, 1975, has been revised in January 1978 and August 1980.

Religion: About 47 percent of the population follows traditional African religions. Roman Catholicism was the official religion when Portugal ruled Angola, and Catholic and Protestant missionaries converted many Angolans to Christianity. Today about 38 percent of Angolans are Roman Catholic and 15 percent Protestant.

Flag: The upper half is red, the lower half black. In the center a five-pointed yellow star and half a yellow cogwheel are crossed by a yellow machete.

Money: The Angolan escudo (AE) was the national currency until 1977 when the kwanza (Kw) replaced it. In 1990 Kw 1 = $0.0334 in United States currency.

Weights and Measures: Angola uses the metric system.

Population: 8,971,000 (1989 estimate); 25 percent urban, 75 percent rural

Cities:
Luanda	1,250,000
Huambo	90,000
Lobito	75,000
Benguela	50,000

(Population based on 1983 estimate.)

GEOGRAPHY

Highest Point: Mt. Moco, 8,596 ft. (2,620 m)

Lowest Point: Sea level along the coast

Rivers: Rivers are numerous, but few are navigable. There are three types: constantly fed rivers (such as the Zaire River); seasonally fed rivers; and temporary rivers and streams. Only the Zaire and the Cuanza, in central Angola, are navigable. The Cuanza is more than 625 mi. (1,006 km) long and flows northward; the Cunene, 590 mi. (949 km) long, flows southward toward the Atlantic.

Mountains: Angola is made up of wholly broad tablelands that range in altitude from 3,000 to 7,000 ft. (914 to 2,134 m).

Climate: Climate varies according to altitude. There are two distinct seasons—wet and dry. The dry season is from May to October. The rainy season begins around November or December and lasts until April. September and October are the warmest months; July and August, the coolest. The average annual temperature is 65° F. to 70° F. (18° C to 21° C).

Greatest Distances: North to south: 850 mi. (1,368 km)
East to west: 800 mi. (1,287 km)

Area: 481,354 sq. mi. (1,246,700 km²)

NATURE

Trees: Palm trees grow in the coastal areas. Tropical woods are found on the highlands north of the Cuanza River, and deciduous trees grown on the Benguela Highlands. The baobab tree is common; it looks as if it were growing upside down.

Animals: Lions, impalas, hyenas, hippopotomuses, rhinoceroses, and elephants are prevalent. The black sable antelope is the most distinctive. Crocodiles are found in many swamps and rivers. The civil war has reduced the number of wildlife.

Fish: Whales, tortoises, and shellfish abound, as do a wide variety of fish—sardines, tuna, carapau, corvina, shad, swordfish, sawfish, and shark.

EVERYDAY LIFE

Housing: Most of the Angolan people live in simple wooden or clay houses. In the towns and villages, however, modern buildings, often Portuguese built, stand in sharp contrast to the shanty towns that dot the periphery.

There is a national housing program, which involves some construction and some attempts at self-help with government plans and materials.

Holidays:

January 1, New Year's Day
January 8, National Culture Day
February 4, Anniversary of Outbreak of Anti-Portuguese Struggle

March 24 to 27, Victory Day
April 14, Youth Day
May 1, May Day
August 1, Armed Forces Day
September 17, National Heroes Day
November 11, Independence Day
December 1, Pioneers Day
December 25, Family Day

Culture: A National Council for Culture has been created to revive and explore native Angolan culture. An Anthropology Museum, a War Museum, and a Slavery Museum have been established.

The sculpture of the Chokwe people is the foremost art form; it is exquisitely carved sculpture that has ritual meaning or practical use. Chokwe basketry, pottery, and beadwork are beautiful.

Modern literature is rich in social and historical overtones. Angola's first president, Agostinho Neto, wrote poetry from his prison cell. Luandino Vieira, Angola's most famous writer, wrote about the underground movement before independence.

In 1978 the *carneval* (carnival), a celebration before Lent (forty days of penitence and fasting preceding Easter), was revived and taken to many parts of the country. It was that carneval that was originally carried to Brazil on slave ships.

The Angola Museum in Luanda contains the national archives and collections on art, history, and zoology. The Dundo Museum, in northeastern Angola, houses collections on ethnography and history.

Sports and Recreation: Soccer is the national sport, but basketball, cycling, swimming, shooting, tennis, and volleyball also are popular.

Communication: All of the media are owned and controlled by the state. The only daily newspaper is the *Jornal de Angola*. The government news sheet is called *Diario da Republica*.

There are about 400,000 radios and 33,000 television sets. Television has two stations that offer many locally produced news and music programs and broadcasts soccer games from countries around the world. There are over 40,000 telephones.

Western films and music are popular. Cinemas exist in all Angolan towns and a mobile cinema tours the rural areas.

Transportation: Because most of the rivers in Angola are unnavigable, railroads have been vital to the development of the interior. There are almost 2,000 miles (3,217 kilometers) of rail lines. The disruption of rail traffic during the war has contributed to Angola's serious economic difficultues.

TAAG (Angola Airlines) is the national airline and it provides both national and international service.

Ports are located at Luanda, Lobita, Namibe, and Cabinda. A ferry service connects Luanda with some of the smaller cities and towns along the northern coast; a new ferry service opened in 1989 linking Luanda with the southern coastal city of Lobito.

Education: The constitution guarantees free education to all, although it is only compulsory for children of elementary school age. The MPLA has taken steps to eradicate illiteracy. Today the literacy rate is about 20 percent.

In 1963 a university was established in Luanda. There are also two Catholic seminaries and several teacher-training schools.

Health and Welfare: The MPLA established a National Health Service in 1975. Civil war and a lack of trained medical personnel have made implementation difficult, however. Malnutrition and poor sanitation have led to widespread disease. Mass immunization campaigns have attempted to battle tropical diseases. Infant mortality is the highest in the world, and the life expectancy for men is only 40 years and for women, 43.

Principal Products:
Agriculture: Coffee, cotton, sisal, maize, beans, sugar, rice, palm kernels, palm oil, tobacco
Mining: Petroleum, diamonds, iron ore, copper ore, manganese, phosphates, salt, gold, bauxite, uranium
Manufacturing: Beer, tires, cement, chemicals, small ships, steel, paper, processing of local crops—fish, sisal, cotton, textiles, and tobacco

IMPORTANT DATES

A.D. 1300—Bantu-speaking, Iron-Age people move into Angola from Central Africa

1483—Portuguese explorers reach Angola

1500—Portugal claims Brazil in South America

1575-1860—Portuguese fight the Mbundu over silver (there was none) and the slave trade. The Mbundu are almost wiped out

1576—Portuguese settlers build fort at Luanda

1580-1680—1,000,000 slaves are taken from Angola, mostly to work on Brazil's sugar plantation, a major element in Portuguese trade

1592—Portuguese establish colonial government in Luanda

1617—Portuguese build a fort at Benguela

1641—Dutch take Luanda

1648—Portuguese recover Luanda

1806—Great Britain outlaws the slave trade

1830-32 — 90 ships come from Brazil to get slaves

1836 — Portugal abolishes the slave trade in its territories

1845 — Fewer than 2,000 whites live in Angola

1858 — Slavery is legally abolished in Angola

1875 — Slaves in Angola are set free

1884 — Berlin Conference honors Portugal's claim to Angola

1920s — Major diamond field is discovered in northeast Angola

1926 — Boundaries of Angola are firmly fixed; dispute with South-West Africa (Namibia) is settled; military dictatorship under Antonio Salazar begins in Portugal

1931 — Benguela Railway is completed

1951 — Angola becomes an official overseas province under Portuguese rule

1956 — MPLA, Popular Movement for the Liberation of Angola, is formed

1959 — Coffee is Angola's chief export crop

1961 — Guerrilla warfare against Portuguese begins

1962 — FNLA, the Front for the Liberation of Angola, is formed

1966 — UNITA, National Union for the Total Independence of Angola, is formed

1974 — Over 330,000 whites are living in Angola

1975 — Angola becomes independent of Portugal on November 11

1976 — Civil war begins

1979 — Agostinho Neto dies; José Eduardo dos Santos becomes president

IMPORTANT PEOPLE

Mário de Andrade (1893-1985), poet, novelist, and essayist

Bernardo de Sá da Bandeira (1795-1876), marques; Portuguese prime minister who abolished the slave trade

Diogo Cão (?-1486), first European to see the Congo River (now the Zaire), in 1483

Leonel Alexander Gomes Cardoso (1919-89), admiral; last Portuguese high commissioner

Antonio Rosa Coutinho (1926-   ), admiral; Portuguese governor of Angola at time of Angolan independence; arranged Cuban support for MPLA

Antão Goncalves, Portuguese sea captain; first to reach West African coast, in 1441

Henry the Navigator (1394-1460), Portuguese prince who encouraged the exploration of the new continent of Africa

Agostinho Neto (1922-79), fighter for Angolan independence; first president, from 1975 to 1979; poet

Nzinga (1582-1663), queen, sister of the king of Ndongo; represented her people in negotiations with the Portuguese

Manuel Pacavira (1939-   ), Angola's ambassador to the United Nations

Holden Roberto (1925-   ), leader of Angolan nationalist group named FNLA

Antonio Salazar (1869-1970), Portuguese dictator; minister of the colonies, in 1930; prime minister of Portugal from 1932 to 1968

Antonio Santos, 1988 Olympic competitor in the triple jump

José Eduardo dos Santos (1942-   ), became president in 1979

Jonas Savimbi (1934-   ), leader of UNITA

Luandino Vieira (1935-   ), Angola's most famous contemporary writer; author of *Luuanda* and *The True Life of Domingos Xavier*; a white Portuguese who started television service in Angola

Robert Williams, Scotsman; financed building of Benguela Railroad

INDEX

Page numbers that appear in boldface type indicate illustrations

127

About the Author

Jason Lauré was born in Chehalis, Washington, and lived in California before joining the United States army and serving in France. He attended Columbia University and worked for *The New York Times*. He traveled to San Francisco and became a photographer during the turbulent 1960s. He recorded those events before setting out on the first of many trips to Africa.

Mr. Lauré covers the political life of that continent and also has made a number of expeditions across the Sahara. He has written about, and photographed in, forty countries in Africa. He has written three books, published by Farrar, Straus & Giroux Inc., on South Africa, Portugal, and Bangladesh, in collaboration with Ettagale Blauer. Their Bangladesh book was nominated for a National Book Award.

In the Enchantment of the World series, Mr. Lauré has written the books on Zimbabwe and Zambia.

Mr. Lauré is married to Marisia Lauré, a translator.